A Guide to Collecting Beer mats

© Ian Calvert 2006

Foreword

I am delighted to have been asked to contribute a foreword to this most interesting and informative piece of work by Ian Calvert. I have known Ian for upwards of twenty-five years, and throughout this entire period of time, his dedication and commitment to further exploring his chosen specialist field of interest, the collecting and documentation of that humble but ubiquitous item, the beer mat, has never wavered. This can most aptly be demonstrated throughout the pages of this book, which is a comprehensive and illuminating product of a labour of love which has endured for more than a quarter of a century.

This book is however much more than a mere tribute to Ian's longstanding and abiding individual passion, the beer mat, whilst doubtless regarded by some simply as a functional and disposable item of brewery and licenced trade ephemera, serves as an important function in depicting the seismic changes that have taken place in the United Kingdom brewing industry since the mats inception in the 1920's. Through the pages of this book can be traced the brewing industry's transformation and metamorphous over much of the preceding century. During this period both the industry and licenced trade have experienced significant and tumultuous changes, with much rationalisation and consolidation post WW2, which today has resulted in an industry and trade dominated by a few big operators. Conversely through this spawned the Beer Orders legislation of the mid 1980's, which lent encouragement to the emergence of a plethora of new small independent breweries, with many of the later resurrecting long forgotten and unfairly neglected beer styles and names.

All this and more is documented and depicted in this most worthy book, which is a most welcome addition to the published works in the field of Breweriana in general.

Charlie McMaster

Scottish Brewing Heritage
June 2006

There's a collector in all of us...

We all collect something... from postcards, stamps, Dinky toys, coins to comics, ornaments etc. There's something in each of us that gives us the collectors instinct. You only need to have a few items but like it or not you're a collector and before long you are hooked with the collecting bug. Before you know it you've got all your friends and relatives bringing you back pieces they've picked up on holiday or bought you for your birthday. What may start as a small number of items soon breed and before you know it you have taken over the spare room or you have considered moving to a larger property.

Being a collector doesn't mean you have to spend a fortune or pick up every issue that's been released. Others diversify or specialise their collections by only concentrating on, for example, manufacturer, region or date.

The collector profile stretches from the casual to the hardcore "must have" (aka obsessed). You may have a casual approach to maintaining your collection whilst there are others who spend all their free time chasing the "latest and greatest". Many people subscribe to collectors societies, mailing lists, specialist interest magazines where they can share their passion with others. Many collectors trawl car boot sales, flea markets or collector's fairs in the hope of finding that elusive issue, bargain or relic. Other collectors sit in the comfort of their homes and search through the internet for information, adverts or articles of interest covering their hobby.

Serious collectors are often termed an "anorak", usually associated with train-spotters. Personally whilst I have been on the receiving end of this label, I often find that once "initiated" these people begin to appreciate the time and effort that's been put in over the years. Their closing statement often ends in "I wish I had a hobby or interest like you" whilst retracting their anorak statement.

Often the collector goes through phases were the interest is short lived and consequently consigned to storage in the loft. These collections may end up as hidden treasure in the loft as it is not unknown for collections to remain undisturbed for decades. On the other hand I can quote several stories about collections retrieved from long term storage to be found soiled by damp or worst case dare I say woodworm.

We all put a value on our collections. In a collectors world it is down to supply and demand. What you pay for it doesn't mean it is worth that. It's simply a question of knowing your limits. I have seen collectors get caught up in the excitement of an auction paying well over the odds for something that in general is relatively common. If you are going to spend money on your collection you need to know its general market value. We have all read articles on someone being fortunate enough to have sold an item at an exorbitant rate knowing full well it's not worth what's being offered. Many people collect objects as an investment in the hope that their piece or copy may be in high demand in years to come.

Value is not necessarily about an items rarity. Often condition out-weighs age. Items in pristine, never used condition will fetch more than those with damage or missing parts. Collectors are on the look out for high quality, well maintained pieces. I have occasionally bought mats in auction to complete the missing gaps in sets or series hoping to "trade on" the duplicates which in return recovers some of my outlay.

Collectors also have to be aware of counterfeit copies. Where there's a high demand market, it's not unusual for modern replicas to appear. This is more prevalent in the antiques market rather than the closer to home small time collectors' arena. Be aware Guinness memorabilia is famous for reproduction copies. Those in the know can pick out the tell tale signs of even a well produced replica but to the less unfortunate you may well be at the end of a scam.

In recent years television has exposed the world of the collector. Television programmes such as "Flog It", "Bargain Hunt" and "Cash in the Attic" have increased awareness of collectable items. This also has a negative side as having seen similar items sell for high prices, people then assume their piece is of similar value and consequently raised prices. I was once reminded of an applicable quote – "all that glitters is not gold". Age does not necessarily mean a higher value. Many items are mass produced and still readily available. The problem the buyer faces is convincing the seller that the article for sale is common and may not be worth the asking price. This can place the buyer in an embarrassing situation appearing as if they are trying to pull a "fast one". In these situations I have always found it best to walk away from the deal.

As your collection grows in stature and size you may find yourself in a predicament whereby you mistakenly buy a duplicate. If you are spending big money on your items this could become an expensive mistake. This is where cataloguing becomes invaluable. By matching what you have against the entries in published catalogues you can then consider marking these items off or on the other hand compile lists (either by noting those you have or those you don't).

Collecting should be fun, after all to most of us it's a pastime. We all go through spates of enthusiasm were you may have some free time to spend on your hobby. It's often too easy to get caught up in something and before you know it the evening is over. Corresponding with other collectors not only allows you to share your interest but develops friendships which can extend beyond your common interest.

I hope that you can relate to some of the above. I have always believed that you get back what you put into your hobby.

Why collect beer mats?

In planning the content of my book the first question that needs addressing is why I collect beer mats? I could simply reply "why not" but that's a politician's answer. In my mind there are several reasons. My interest stretches from the historical angle through to what I often consider to be small pieces of art work. We all collect something be it dust or memories.

I started collecting in 1976 when I picked up my first mat off a pub table whilst helping my father on his delivery van distributing wines and spirits to pubs, clubs and off-licences during the school holidays. I joined the British Beermat Collectors Society (BBCS) in Feb 1977, in the prime of my youth. Too young at the time to drink in pubs I discovered the Societies existence through an advert in the Exchange and Mart paper. Having sent off my joining fee, I promptly received my first magazine, Society membership mat, the Guide to Tegestology handbook and a Society enamel lapel badge. A few weeks' later local collector (and now long time friend) Dennis Harle called at my house to introduce himself. When he left it felt as if I had robbed him, having probably increased my collection by a further one thousand mats. I think Dennis may have picked up one or two from me out of courtesy. I am sure he did it not to embarrass me with not really having anything he needed! I also discovered that there were a few other beer mat collectors in my school which led to a few trading sessions.

My interest in collecting grew when I was old enough to drink (legally) in pubs. My collection encompassed all sorts of issues – UK brewery, foreign, foreign beers in UK, whisky, vodka, cigarettes, airline, trade etc. Furthermore my interest in collecting Breweriana soon expanded to labels, pump clips, books etc. I joined various other related Societies – Brewery History Society, Labologists, The Campaign for Real Ale (CAMRA), Scottish Brewing Archive as well as subscribing to various brewery publications. Fundamentally out of these activities I have gained a sound knowledge of the brewery industry. Presently I have approx. 22,000 UK Brewery mats in my collection dating back as early as 1929.

In recent years, I feel collecting has become more difficult as there's more breweries turning to using mats as a promotional item. Whilst this is good news for the collector, tracking them down can be difficult task. Some breweries have a restricted budget and may only produce small quantities. With support from SIBA, smaller breweries are now seeing real value in using beer mats as promotional rather than functional. In some cases the larger breweries contract outside agencies and distributors to manage their promotions and therefore may not even see the mats in their stores. Some mats are found or reported too late, and therefore collectors have little hope of ever obtaining a copy. Some breweries will not respond to postal requests, participate in the Society organised schemes, or indeed some even go out of their way to make things difficult for collectors. To be fair they have a business to run and collectors may be low on their list of priorities.

On a positive note, I love collecting beer mats, or Tegestology to give the hobby its proper title. I enjoy the chase of the recent mat, the arrival of the postman, the unexpected e-mail, the grapevine gossip as to "what's out there" and I have many great friends who I regularly correspond with.

This book and my website provide an ideal platform to exhibit my collection. I have tried to cover all aspects of collecting but since my interest is in the UK brewery scene it is predominantly focused towards this area but I have included others as examples. Apologies if your favourite mat or brewery is not featured within the book (volume 2?). All the mats illustrated within this book are from my collection unless otherwise stated.

www.calvert-beermats.com

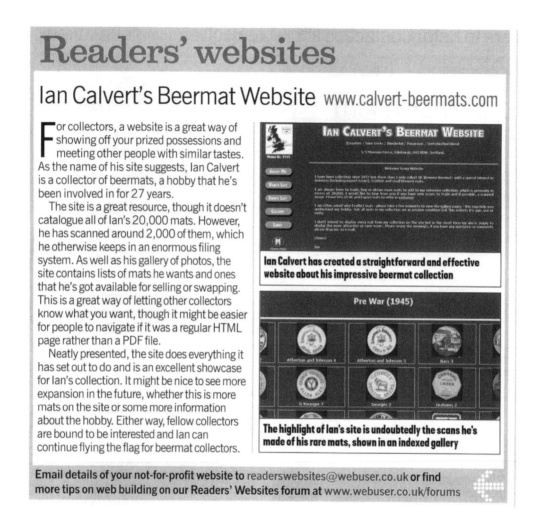

Each mat has a story as to how it was obtained. Whilst I do view myself as one of the "hardcore" members I do appreciate that there's more serious things in life and dare I say it I will never have all the listed mats. None the less this is part of the fun. Please remember that at the end of the day, beer mats are only bits of cardboard initially produced to advertise products and to absorb your spilt beer.

May I also take this opportunity to thank everyone who has helped pull this book together especially Dennis Harle and Ian Mackay. The role of honour would not be complete without thanking Alison Keogh, Chris Bolton and David Akroyd at the Katz Group for access to their premises, knowledge and time but more importantly for their support and sponsorship of this book. Additionally a big thank you to everyone, who over the years has taken the time and trouble to pick up mats for me on their travels.

I shall finish on this note – I am often asked, "What is my favourite beer mat in my collection?" – There's only ever been one answer – "*THE NEXT ONE*".

Definitions

Breweriana – The collecting, preservation, study and history of advertising within the brewing industry

Tegestology – Name given to the study and collection of beer mats

Tegestologist – A collector of beer mats. Derived from the Latin word "teges" which means small rug or mat.

Beer mat (also known as coasters, drip mats, bar mats) – A beer mat is a piece of woodpulp board (or other material) used on pub tables to sit your glasses of beer (or other alcoholic beverages) upon. They are used not just to protect the surface of the table, but, as they are usually made out of paper, they can also be used to absorb spillages. Their main usage, however, is as part of an advertising campaign. Beer mats are usually adorned with a customized image – usually advertising a brand of beer, although they can also be used to promote a drinking establishment, sports franchise, or special event, the list is endless. Although they appear to be a disposable item, in fact they are quite durable and reusable.

Flimsy – A cocktail style mat manufactured from light paper. Often found in hotel bars.

Drop catcher – similar to a flimsy but has a slit in the design to allow the mat to wrap around the stem of the glass to absorb condensation droplets

Export – Reference to a mat issued in another country out with of the UK

Joint advertising – A mat commissioned by brewery in conjunction with another company ie; Guinness & Bass

Over print – A mat privately commissioned to overlay additional information on top of original mat

Tandem– Mat advertising two different products ie; brewery and a pub company.

Giant/Mega – Associated with mats above 15cm in size (diameter or radius). Often used on bars rather than on tables.

Private issue – this is where a collector has commissioned a print on the blank side of a general issue (often advertising collectors meetings)

Unlisted issue – a mat currently not listed within the BBCS catalogues

Variation – mat found with slight variations from original listed entry

Previous books on Tegestology

Over the years as my interest in my hobby increased so did my knowledge about the subject. I felt it would be appropriate to share this information in the hope that it is of interest to new collectors as well as those established collectors looking for reference material.

As I write this book there is currently little information available on the subject and felt that there is sufficient demand and interest to encourage me to undertake this project. The last serious book to cover the subject was released in 1979 and other more recent books on beer or Breweriana have not given the topic adequate coverage.

When I joined the British Beermat Collectors Society I received an enamel badge and an official handbook titled "The beer drinkers guide to Tegestology" (fig 1). At the time this was the definitive collectors guide. Unfortunately this handbook has not been updated which in part spurred me to producing this book. The odd copy of this book occasionally appears for sale on the E-bay auction website.

In 1979 Brian Pipe & Keith Osborne produced a hardback book titled "The International Book of Beer Labels, Mats & Coasters"[1]. This book is still in common circulation today. The book provides a good insight to collecting with many pictures of mats and labels.

Another book worthy of mention is Keith Wilson's "An introduction to Breweriana (a study of British breweries advertising relics)"[2]. This book as the title states covers the wide range of collectable brewery items. Keith later produced a further book titled "Commemorative Breweriana a study of special issues"[3]. Martyn Cornell's book "Beer Memorabilia"[4] published in 2000 gave the subject a favourable seventeen pages. Other books on beer have briefly mentioned mat collecting with only a few mats displayed. Often the mats portrayed are generally quite common. One aim I hope to achieve in this book is to include photographs of more scarce mats. Whilst every mat in my collection may not be in the best condition I feel that the inclusion of the odd beer-stained or slightly damaged (pin holes etc) adds to the reality factor highlighting their original purpose ie; soak up the spilt beer.

Figure 1

[1] ISBN 0 600 31474 Published in 1979 by Hamlyn
[2] ISBN 0 9507495 09 Published in 1981
[3] ISBN 0 9507495 16 Published in 1985
[4] ISBN 1-84092-214-1 Published in 2000 by Apple

History of the Beer Mat

In the late 19th century beer was cheap and was drunk by people of all classes. It was essentially home brewed and varied significantly in taste and strength. This variation may in part be due to the cleanliness of the water supply.

The higher classes drank from pewter tankards whilst the poorer made do with clay or wooden drinking vessels. The rich had elaborate personal designs embossed or engraved into their tankard, many also had lids. Felt mats were used to sit on top of the vessels that did not have lids to protect the drink from insects, dust etc. Given that these felt mats were absorbent they were also used to wipe up spilt beer. Being made of material these protective lids could be washed and used again. The felt material soon became unhygienic as they harboured bacteria and began to smell.

In 1880 the first cardboard mat was produced by Robert Sputh. In 1892 he patented his procedure (No.68499) for the production of wood pulp beer mats. The process involved casting paper pulp into moulds which were left to dry overnight. The beer mats had a diameter of 107 mm and a thickness of 5 mm. The absorbent and hygienic cardboard discs manufactured in the Sputh mill near Sebnitz in Germany fast became generally accepted in preference to the felt mats. These mats tended to be plain, printed on one side only and of one colour.

The beer mat also has its origins in the pottery coasters that were placed under mugs of mulled ale to protect the surfaces of inn tables in the 19th century. These coasters advertised the names of breweries or their trademarks. Whilst this practice in Britain appeared to have continued until after the First World War on the continent of Europe things were different. Here the paper manufacturers developed a wood pulp board that was cheap, highly absorbent and provided a good surface for printing.

The UK had to wait until 1922 to see the first mats appearing on pub tables. The earliest mats known for an English brewery were issued by Watney, Combe, Reid & Co Ld. The mats were copies of two bottle labels – Watney's Pale Ale and Reid's Stout (fig 2 & 3).

Figure 2

Figure 3

However, mats were used fourteen years before this, although not in connection with brewery products. An American illusionist, whose stage name was Chung Ling Soo was touring British theatres in the summer of 1908. The highlight of his act was "Condemned to Death by the Boxers" in which he survived being shot by a firing squad at point-blank range. This was ultimately the cause of his death a few years later when the act went wrong. Mats were printed for performances in at least two of the theatres.

The earliest mats were individually stamped using the letterpress process. The mats were printed in one colour and on one side only. The manufacturing process soon became industrialised by 1895 using fibre-cast materials. In the 1920's colours were introduced and the breweries soon issued coloured mats in greater numbers to advertise their beers.

With an increased demand the manufacturing process was updated in 1928 when Katz (Germany) developed a semi-automatic printing machine capable of printing more than one colour at once and in higher volumes. These machines were in use up until the 1970's. The majority of mats printed between 1922 and 1939 had the printers name on them which today helps collectors in dating mats. During World War II mat production ceased although one issue by Offilers of Derby is known to have been printed during this period.

As demand increased further, and with improved technology Katz developed a combined letterpress and stamping machine. These machines (known as BDS) allowed cardboard to run through a series of rollers which produced printed stamped mats as the cardboard emerged through to the other end of the machine. These machines were in general production up until 1984.

At the same time Katz installed a Fourdrinier cardboard machine. This machine, the first of its kind continuously produced so-called Fourdrinier cardboard in 1.5mm to 2.5mm thicknesses from sheets or rolls.

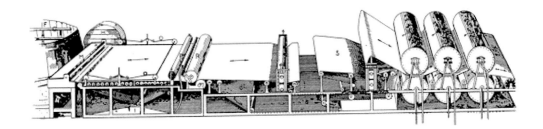

In the late 1970's the machinery could not keep pace with the high demand and as a result multi-coloured offset printing was introduced. Entire sheets of cardboard were printed from which individual mats were then cut or stamped out.

As printing technology improved over the years so did the raw materials used to produce mats. Today's mats are printed on high quality white absorbent pulp board. This is achieved by sandwiching the pulp board between two thin sheets of white paper (bleached board).

The standard and most economical size Drip/Beer Mat is 89mm square (with 6mm radius cut corners) with 1.4mm thickness. Lithography is now the industry standard and is more commonly used for larger quantities. The process is highly effective for printing fine-detail designs and photographs.

Quarmby based in Huddersfield are the leading European manufacturer of beer mats (part of the Katz Group with offices in Belgium, a print factory and pulpboard mill in Germany). John Quarmby started his business in West Riding in the 1870's selling paper bags in the streets from the back of a hand cart. His products soon took off and he expanded his business by employing a boy to take over the deliveries then by employing his elder son as a partner. He obtained premises in Huddersfield and from here he started to manufacture bags. The business continued to expand and he moved to larger premises in 1912 but on the day of the Titanic disaster the factory was destroyed by fire. John rebuilt the premises and decided to concentrate on the making of cardboard boxes.

In 1931 he installed his first beer mat printing machine. This soon became a success and over the course of the last 75 years Quarmby has become the world leader in printing mats. In the Huddersfield plant Quarmby print an average of three million mats per day. Today Quarmby offer other promotional items including ashtrays, playing cards, clocks... the list goes on.... Always keen to introduce new lines and initiatives to gain competitive edge, the Katz Group have extended the use of the beer mat beyond its origins, re-inventing it into different formats, including new lines designed for use out with the drinks industry.

Beermat Production

The majority of beer mats are produced using offset lithography. This works on a very simple principle: ink and water don't mix. Images (graphics and text) are put on aluminium plates which are dampened first by water, then ink. The ink adheres to the image area, the water to the non-image area. The image is then transferred to a rubber blanket and from the rubber blanket to the beer mat board. The term offset refers to the fact that the image isn't printed directly to the paper from the plates, but is offset or transferred to another surface that then makes contact with the board. Unlike other forms of printing, in offset lithography the image on the printing plate is not recessed or raised.

Before the job can be printed, the approved graphics must be converted to film or aluminium "plates." Film negatives are created from digital files. Images from the negatives are transferred to printing plates directly from the film or these days computer hence the term "Computer to Plate (CTP)"

At the design stage the overall plate layout is calculated to obtain the maximum number of mats per board to minimise costs and waste. Each of the primary colours – black (key), cyan (blue), magenta (red), and yellow has a separate plate. There are occasions when 6 plates may be used for example in matching specific Pantone colours

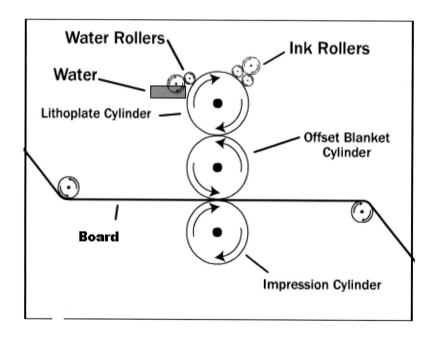

The four ink colours are Cyan (Blue), Magenta (Red), Yellow and Black (key) – often referred to as CMYK. Because the inks used are translucent, they can be overprinted and combined in a variety of different proportions to produce a wide range of colours based upon a printer's pantone guide. Pantone is a standardized colour identification system for selecting, specifying, matching, and controlling colours. The Pantone system defines mixes of base inks, and is called spot colours.

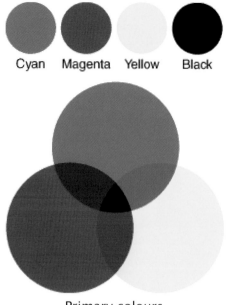

Cyan   Magenta   Yellow   Black

Primary colours

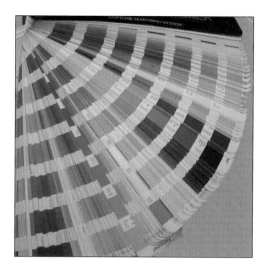

Pantone colour guide

Theoretically it is possible to produce an adequate range of colours using just Cyan, Magenta and Yellow. The black plate is used to strengthen the shadow areas and reduce the amount of CMY inks required.

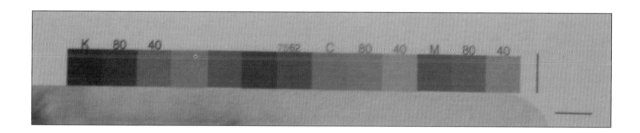

Each board has colour bars printed around the top and bottom edges for visual quality control The band shows the various shades of the four colours based upon the weight of the ink (ie; solid, 80%, 40% etc). The operator uses an eye-glass to manually view the colour match. The mix of the inks is controlled by an electronic panel but the machine operator can manually adjust the flow using a series of buttons on the printing machine at each colour deck.

Additionally "tick marks" are printed at the edges along to assist with alignment (horizontally and vertically). These marks are used later for accurate alignment when the mats are individually punched out.

Designs & Artwork

If you are considering having a beer mat produced here are a number of things you may need to consider

- Target Audience
- Promoting brand or products
- Design & layout (front & reverse)
- Quantity
- Budget allowance or constraints
- Launch or delivery date requirements
- Size of mat *
- Shape
- Set or series
- Number of colours
- Material (Board, Bleached, Wood pulp, Cork, Thin card etc)
- Laminated
- Embossed
- Value added process (heat sensitive, scratch panels, foil embossing, holographic)

* Standard size of mats –

89mm square 6mm corner radius or 89mm circle
or
95mm square 6mm corner radius or 95mm circle

Once you have defined your requirements you can sketch up some initial designs for the printer to work with. The printers will accept designs in most formats on compact disk (jpeg/bmp etc) Recommended resolution is 300 pixels per inch for scanned images.

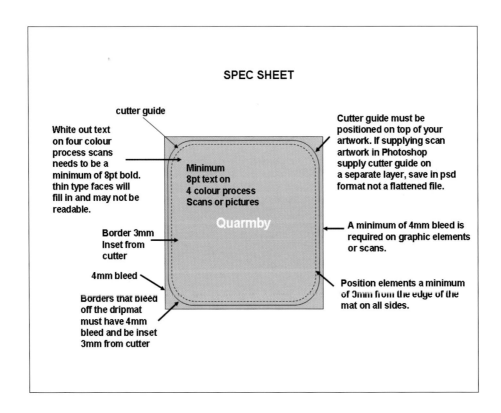

Print Process

All beer mats start life with the customer having a concept or particular requirement in mind.

The production process is generally as follows

1. **Enquiry** – initially the customer will request information on pricing and delivery dates. Information such as a standard price guide, a company profile and some samples are supplied to the customer. Quarmby have a standard price list which quotes print runs from 5,000 to 25,000 for a standard 95mm square or circular mat printed on both sides.

2. **Quotation** – Once the customer has a clear definition of their requirements a formal quotation will be issued. Additional options may include bespoke packaging, enhancements such as adding scratch off panels or a cutter for an unusual shape.

3. **Order** – once the customer is satisfied that all their requirements have been defined a purchase order is required prior to starting any work.

4. **Creative Studio** – the customer will be requested to provide the artwork in electronic format. Subject to the size of the files they are either received on a compact disk or received electronically via e-mail. Upon receipt the Art Studio staff will confirm that all the files are present and can be read. Due to incompatibility issues between Apple Mac pc's and Microsoft Windows the most common problem encountered relates to fonts. The original files are kept for reference. Having confirmed that all the files are present (graphics, text, fonts and other elements), the studio staff will use various software tools to produce the required design. The design will incorporate any special features requested by the customer in addition to calculating the maximum number of mats printed per sheet of board. This will then be passed over to the "production team" to work on.

5. **Proof Samples** – The proof can be in a number of formats;

   - A small print run will be produced on board (known as a wet proof). These are printed on a conventional proof press resulting in an excellent representation of the final product.
   - A digital proof will be created on board material showing cutter profile, colour and register. Although this proof is not printed on a conventional press it is made up with the same elements. Half-tone dots can be seen showing extremely close colour accuracy to the final beer mat.
   - An Adobe Portable Document Format (PDF) file will be created. These are for content approval only and cannot be used for exact colour matching as they do not take in to account the production process. Jobs approved in this format will be matched to standard ink weights, ensuring good quality production at all times.

If wet proofs are required smaller sized printing plates are ordered. These plates will be used on the smaller scale printing machine. This press works slightly differently from the larger scale production machines in that only one colour is applied at a time ie; each colour is applied separately. The inks dry relatively quickly as the board material absorbs the ink. The process requires that the machine operator must wash down the press between each colour. The proofs are then sent to the customer with a form asking for approval. Regardless of proof format the customer will be asked to sign-off the design. It is the customer's responsibility to check all spelling and colour matches.

6. Scheduling – Once the customer has approved the design the plates are ordered (these are out sourced). The production manager will then evaluate all current and pending orders and update the manufacturing schedule. Planning is an important task and must consider customer commitments, stock levels of materials (ink, board, plates, and cutters).

7. Print production – Prior to a scheduled print run, Quarmby will ensure that the required details are fully understood by the production staff and that all the required materials are in stock. The job specification worksheet is passed between departments as the production progresses (ie; print, cut and packaging). When the production is complete the worksheet documents are then stored away with samples for future reference ie; for a reprint.

The job specification sheet includes details such as

- Customer information (name, design reference, terms etc)
- Production information (quantity, board layout, material spec, print spec, cutting packaging information etc)

The print process is as follows

- If necessary the rollers are cleaned to clear any build up of fibres and dust from previous runs
- The guides will be set to ensure the print will be in line (fig 4). Each plate is held in place with clamps all of which require precise alignment at each of the four (or six) decks to ensure the board is printed accurately. The plates will be fitted and aligned in the correct sequence into the four printing decks. An adjustment of up to 2mm can be controlled via manual controls at the side of each deck unit. There is no room for error as any misalignment will result in printing in the wrong area resulting in an incorrect register of the colours.
- The pallet holding the sheets of board will be loaded in the feeder end
- A number of boards will be run off and checked for alignment and colour matching
- Following any minor adjustments the print run will commence

The ink is fed from the drums (fig 5) to the press via a series of overhead pipes into the ink rollers. The water is chilled having had alcohol and a chemical additive (called Fountain) added, then piped into the troughs on each dock unit.

Figure 4

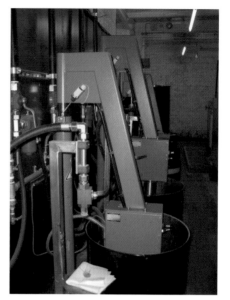

Figure 5

The run is constantly monitored by the operators to ensure quality is maintained throughout the run. All colours are applied on one pass as the board passes through the press. The colours are printed in the following sequence (assuming the design setup is based on CMYK)

1. Deck 1 – black
2. Deck 2 – cyan
3. Deck 3 – magenta
4. Deck 4 – yellow

There may be occasions where the black is loaded last, usually to enhance the quality of the end product.

Figure 6

As batches of completed boards stack up on the output feeder (known as the delivery end), the full pallet is moved to one side (queued up for printing on the second side or ready for cutting) (fig 6). The control panel has a counter display to assist the operator achieving an average stack height. The print run continues during the transfer to a new pallet (the continuous stack built up during the change over is held temporarily with roller bars controlled by the operator via the panel buttons) (fig 7).

Other control panels display the production statistics such as the number of boards completed per hour. This aids management in calculating production run times. Mats with designs on both sides are turned with care taken to ensure that when printed the second side is printed the correct way up.

Figure 7

8. **Cut out** – during the design stage consideration is given to the required shape and size. Anything that is non standard may require special handling. The cutting board (a pallet like design with manufactured foamed padded shapes on one side inset with blades to punch out the shape) is included within the price.

Figure 8

Once the print run is complete the output pallets are queued for cutting.

This is a simple process:

- The pallet is loaded in the input feeder (fig 8)
- Each board is grabbed by the grippers and rolled through the guides
- The cutting board is timed to punch down on the board as it passes through
- The next step punches out the individual mats from the board
- Each punched mat falls into a stack on top of a pallet into predetermined stack sizes (fig 9)
- The remainder of the board is then rolled out at the far end into a waste pile (fig 10)
- The completed pallet of punched out mats are then queued for packaging

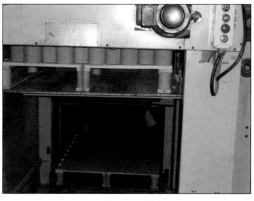

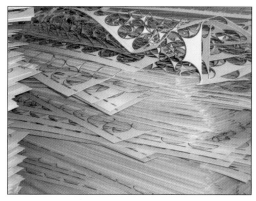

Figure 9	Figure 10

9. **Packaging** – this is customer specific. Mats can either be stacked or sealed in pre-determined, variable sizes or in multi packs containing 1,000 mats as requested by the customer. Mats are placed on a mechanical roller which directs the batch into a small oven which heat seals the polythene around the pile (fig 11). The shrink-wrapped pack then continues down the line to either be packed onto a pallet or placed into boxes. The finished product is then taken to the dispatch area.

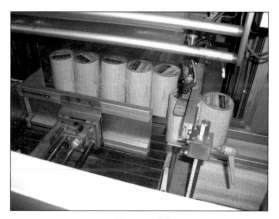

Figure 11

10. **Distribution** – subject to the order quantity the orders will either be delivered direct to the customer on pallets or dispatched by couriers

10. **Miscellaneous** – additional extras such as embossing with varnish or scratch panels are completed in-house using screen print printing presses.

The Environment

Billions of beer mats are printed each year. These mats have a short lifespan before being disposed off. The printers have an awareness of the environment. As trees are felled and forests vanish in high numbers throughout the world, printers welcome initiatives and participate in measures to reduce environmental waste. Calculations defined at the planning stage ensure the maximum number of mats in each sheet of board whilst minimising waste. Advances in technology have significantly impacted on minimizing waste. For example:

- Production of artwork or designs can be transferred electronically reducing the use of external media such as compact disks and the consequent postage and packaging
- Conventional plates involved the production of film, analogue proofing and then plate processing – each requiring their own chemical process. Computer to plate (CTP) or digital plates are made from 100% aluminium and any damaged or scrap items are recycled.
- Beer mat board is produced from wood–pulp. The pulp is constructed from a mix of already recycled paper pulp and softwood.
- Inks containing renewable source resins and vegetable oils are used where ever possible
- The waste from the mat cut–outs are collected and recycled
- Mats are packed with polyethylene film which is easy to recycle and burns without any residues

Board characteristics

- Made of pure spruce wood
- Absorptive strength 50 mg water within 12 seconds
- No glue, bleach, heavy metals or toxins
- Cardboard sheets are up to 1000 mm wide and 1500 mm long, deliverable as machine format and or cuts
- Front and backside are also deliverable in white colour
- Excellent printing characteristics and thus brilliant printed colours and even very fine details
- High absorbency – beer mat absorbs up to 300% of its own weight
- Rapid liquid absorption – no liquid "remains" on the beer mat
- Absolute straightness – beer mats do not bend even after absorbing liquid
- Firm edges – the edges of the beer mat do not crumble away

The Marketing Tool

What is a beer mat?

Essentially a beer mat is a piece of cardboard (or similar material) used to promote awareness, sell a product or relay a message. It also has a practical side absorbing spillages and drips of condensation that runs down the side of the glass. Mats are not just designed for use on pub tables – they can be placed in a multitude of environments. The message can be widely distributed to a wider audience outside of the pub.

Traditionally the domain of the breweries, the beer mat has come of age as is now regarded as an indispensable, important marketing instrument and high impact advertising tool. Well over a billion beer mats are produced around the world every year and beer mats are probably the longest standing marketing tool known to man.

Beer mats are more versatile now that ever before. Mats come in many shapes and sizes and are only restricted by the boundaries of printing machinery. Modern day technology allows multi-colour, textured or eye catching gimmicks designed to capture your attention even if just for a fleeting moment. Companies have used mats in campaigns, competitions, product launches, to enhance their company image or to inform customers about products and services.

Marketing research has reflected a change of emphasis in the role of the beer mat. It has been proven that mats can reach a wider audience than other alternatives such as flyers, banners, posters or similar promotional items. This contrasts from previous views that considered mats primary function was to mop up spillages rather than its advertising potential. This shift is reflected in the fact that mats are no longer used to advertise just drinks, snack foods etc. Mats are now used to advertise any product or event.

Cheap to produce and to distribute mats are ideal as point of sale material. Mats can be used to launch a brand campaign. People buy what they recognise and a familiar logo can often sway the consumer. Research shows that customers choose brands they know in preference to those they do not and qualitative research has proved that a visual image can more quickly identify a brand than text can. Large corporations, small companies, charities and individuals have learned this, and this is why they go through the lengthy process of adopting a logo. The sharp increase in the last thirty years in the use of logos – and in the number of companies that research and design them – illustrates that the business world is satisfied that logos repay all the effort that goes into designing them. There is no guaranteed return on investment, however, the fact that you are promoting your brand, logo and product means it may be recognised the next time and consequently be bought in preference to another less known brand.

Mats have a short life. Placed on tables and bars there use is two fold – to portray a message to the customer and secondly to absorb spilt beer. Often picked up as a souvenir, a reminder of the pub you frequented during a holiday, a reminder of good times. Some end up in people's pockets, under table legs to stabilise wobbly tables whilst others end up stained, cracked, ripped or wet and are only fit for the bin.

Numerous marketing studies have highlighted the potential and effective use of beer mats as an advertising medium

- Guaranteed impact – eye catching
- Promote product awareness
- Low cost-variable sizes of print runs to suit budget
- Beermat advertising has been used for more than 100 years
- Beer mats are in front of the public 24 hours a day, 7 day's a week, every week!
- Beer mats have an average life span of 4-6 weeks!
- Beer mats are part of customary table culture
- More than 500 potential customers will read EACH Beermat
- Conveys many messages, presents a wide variety of information
- Great for product launches, product promotions or just a product reminder
- Ideal for special events, fund raiser, direct mail programmes, trade shows, seminars and conferences
- Perfect for restaurants, nightclubs, pubs, lounges and resorts/hotels
- High quality product that provides an inexpensive means of advertising
- Intricate creative designs, sizes, shapes and colours
- Not considered intrusive (unlike mail shots)
- Entertaining, decorative and original
- Only constrained by the size of the board
- Lightweight – cheap to distribute
- Recyclable and biodegradable
- Mats are ranked 2nd in popularity to cinema advertising

Mats come in various shapes, sizes and materials. Wood pulp is by far the most popular although it is not uncommon to find:

- Flimsy – these are also known as cocktail mats or drop catchers. They are made up of several thin layers of paper. Drop catchers have a slit across the mat to allow it to sit on the stem of the glass to catch condensation droplets.
- Plastic – not to be confused with pump clips which are used on pump handles
- Leather – these tend to be used to promote commercial companies and brands
- Cork – a popular base often used with laminated top surface
- Rubber – a number of 1930 mats were issued in rubber
- Thin card – cheap to produce but often not suitable to soak up beer spills
- Pliadek – issued in limited numbers by breweries in the 1950's and 60's. Manufactured by Pliadek Ltd in Baildon, they used short lengths of coloured nylon or rayon fibre giving a felt like appearance. These were expensive to produce and did not last long as they quickly disappeared into collectors hands.

Various eye catching enhancements have been used in conjunction with the above materials, most popular include

- The use of gold leaf or foils
- Scratch panels (often used for instant prize competitions)
- Laminated varnish finish giving the mat a glossy feel
- Hot or cold spot (temperature sensitive)

Agencies & Promotions Companies

These types of business act as the middle man between the prospective buyer and the printer. These agencies also offer "value-add" services such as design or market research and may involve producing "mock up/proof" examples. For example a brewery may not have its own marketing department or may wish to employ a professional services company to design an advertisement campaign for the launch of a new brand or product. Armed with a few conceptual ideas from the buyer the agency will draw up some initial drafts for evaluation. Once approved the agency will provide the printer with the approved artwork, agree pricing, distribution & delivery schedules etc. The development in technology has reduced the design times as proofs are now produced using computer graphics allowing the customer and the designer to view and modify images.

The number of breweries using agencies has increased significantly in recent years. It can prove cost effective to out-source these requirements as companies do not have to employ specialist staff (marketing & design). Sales teams are best placed out on the road – selling beer into the market.

Some agencies offer storage facilities so that when orders are complete they are delivered and stored in pre-arranged facilities. The service may also include distribution to pubs, clubs etc. Often mats are included in promotional packs and may be packaged along side glasses, bunting, advertising tents, posters etc. The delivery of these promotional packs may be tied to the launch date, competition or campaign.

There are numerous promotions companies in the UK. They offer a wide range of products and services. It is not my intension to list any of these but using any web search engine will return pages of listings.

Proofs

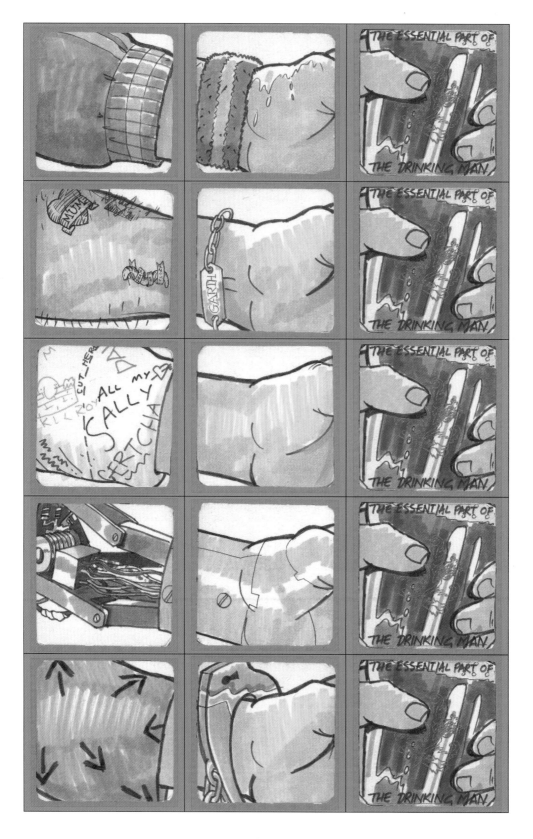

Courtesy of Dennis Harle

These examples produced by Drybrough's following the success of a similar series

Collecting Sources

Collectors Societies

The British Beer mat Collectors Society was formed in 1960. Membership details and benefits are contained within this book. Other collectors societies associated with Breweriana are listed in the appendices section. The Society offers members recent mats for sale in addition to a members advert section. Older rarer mats are auctioned at Society arranged meetings.

Visit your local pub

Not only do you get to sample the beers on tap but you can also pick up any new mats. It's often best to ask the bar staff for some mats as not only do you get clean unused mats often they may have others which are presently not on display. It's common courtesy to ask rather than to clear the tables.

Over the years I have had varied success ranging from being provided with one copy of the mat to a whole pack. Occasionally upon requesting mats I have been told to help myself to mats off the tables. It's not unknown for me to ask (aka disturb) if I could have the mat presently being used at an occupied table. I have found that after a few visits (on my pre planned pub crawl) the landlords have put mats aside for me. Without trying to seem greedy, I ask for several copies of the mat (if supplies allow) the others being for my core of friends that I regularly exchange with.

On several occasions whilst enquiring about mats, I been informed that the pub did have a few packs but they were thrown out in the bins (yes, you have guessed it – I have gone out and raked through the rubbish in the hope of retrieving the disposed packets). Some breweries charge the pubs for supplying mats and are therefore reluctant to hand them out to collectors. Other publicans quote having asked the brewery sales reps for a regular supply of mats but despite promises they never appear.

Whilst personally I only collect mats from UK breweries, one lesson learnt over the years is to refuse nothing. If offered take it – I simply pass these on to other collectors. Furthermore in refusing the landlords offer he may not be so generous the next time you ask.

Beer festivals

This is a great source for obtaining new mats. These events are well organised and you usually find there's a wide range of beers (and mats) to be found. CAMRA run these festivals throughout the year all over the country and are advertised on their website as well as being listed in their monthly newspaper "What's Brewing". Occasionally some festivals are restricted to members only or by advanced ticket sales. The festivals are usually very popular and indeed it's not unknown for all the beer to run out early. Mats are often randomly distributed across the tables and bars. Again it does not go a miss to ask if there's any others currently not out on display.

Write to breweries

This is a good method for obtaining new mats however please bear in mind that a brewery is a business and responding to requests from collectors is a low priority. Courteous letters requesting copies of their latest mats often gets a response but remember to include a suitably sized stamped address envelope. Furthermore I have found that including a small donation to cover costs or as a donation to a local charity is more likely to return a response. Some breweries offer mats for sale on their website.

Brewery visits

Many breweries offer guided tours. Subject to the size of the brewery these are normally formal conducted tours taking the visitor through the brewing process. There are many Health & Safety aspects that the brewery has to be conscious of to ensure there are no mishaps during the walk around. The tour often ends with a few beers in the hospitality of the sample room (also known as "the tap"). These tours tend to be scheduled when the brewing activity for the day quietens down. Some breweries welcome visitors in pre-arranged tours. There are occasions when visitors turn up unannounced and it's really down to the brewer to decide if his/her time can be afforded. To the collector these visits often offer the opportunity to ask for some mats to add to their collections. You may find mats in use in the sample room but it is still best to ask if it is okay to take a copy (or two). Furthermore some brewers stock their mats on site and if time and access is available (these rooms tend to be under lock and key) the brewer may be able to supply other mats currently not being used.

Exchange with other collectors

The internet has opened up a whole new world to the collector. Simply type "beer mats" into any search engine and there's a host of sites listed from printers, collectors sites as well as news articles. The internet has given the collector the ideal forum to display their collections. I have found that through my website I have very positive feedback in regard of the gallery content. The site has also brought offers to exchange mats with collectors worldwide. Another tried and tested way to increase your collection is to correspond with other collectors by sending regular packs of recent local mats. They in turn will respond with new mats from their local breweries. The only cost involved here is postage.

Car Boot Sales

Many areas hold regular car boot sales often held in outdoor areas such as playing fields or in car parks. People recognise that there may be some value in disused items which may have been left abandoned in the loft, garage or under the stairs. Some events charge the seller for their pitch, albeit a car parking space or fold away tables. Monies raised generally cover the cost for stewards and for the hire of the field, hall etc. These events often start quite early in the morning and for those willing to get out of their beds early enough, some choice pickings and the odd bargain are on offer. These events offer sellers a quick return, cash in hand for a days work.

With respect to the collector it is down to your luck on the day. You may have to either ask the stall holder or dig through boxes of junk in the hope of finding hidden treasure. I have had little luck in this area however on the other hand I have picked up some nice items of Breweriana (playing cards, trays etc).

E-bay

E-bay is the largest online auction website in the world. It enables people to sell or buy almost anything on the site (subject to various terms and conditions). The site has a presence within Europe, America and Asia. Sellers and buyers must initially register themselves in their home country, you will be allocated an identity (user name) allowing you to log on and use the service. The seller can offer the goods to bidders either restricted to within their home country or worldwide. The buyer in most cases pays for the postage or shipping of the goods and may be offered insurance.

As a seller you promote your items for sale by completing numerous template forms which steps you through the process to prepare your advert. Once you have reviewed your posting you submit it into the system for the world to view. You can offer the goods for sale based upon either a number of days posting or with a "buy it now" option which offers the goods directly at a higher price (assuming that no one has offered any bids on the item).

All bids are legally binding and buyers and sellers can provide feedback on the sale. This forum allows both buyers and sellers the confidence that previous sales have concluded successfully or if there have been issues (non payment, goods did not arrive, damaged or not as described). On the whole, 99% of all sales are successful. E-bay has a complaints department and can ban users for fraudulent deals, misuse, non-payment etc.

Goods for sale are placed in categories (music, toys, electrical). Beer mats are classified under the Breweriana or collectors sections. Users can search by a text string ie; beermats or beer mats. It is not unusual for sellers to misspell goods (ie; Guiness/Guinnes) and these items often go unsold or picked up on the cheap by the experienced users who have the knowledge to look for these types of errors.

In respect to beer mats, e-bay offers an excellent choice. Many people have found this a quick cheap method of selling either individually, batches or whole collections. I have noticed over the years that seller's expectations have risen having noticed other previously successful high value sales. This has led to over inflated bid start prices. Many items are often described as "rare" or "vintage" when in fact the items in question are still commonly available. As with any item, what you are willing to pay for it may not necessarily be what it is worth when you come to sell it. It's a question of supply and demand. The genuine rare mats often have a starting reserved price or are marked up to a starting price which if sold at would be a realistic value.

E-bay offers a downloadable toolbar for your internet browser which provides tools to manage your account with reminders, bid status etc. Other companies offer "bid snipping" tools which allows you, the bidder, to automatically submit a bid within the last few remaining seconds prior to closure. I have been on the receiving end of a few very late bids some of which outbid my maximum bid price. Sat in front of a pc in the last few moments of a bid closing can be very exciting.

I have found that e-bay is an excellent platform to buy mats but please remember as a collector there are many other ways of adding mats to your collection that does not necessarily involve spending money.

Flea Markets

These events are often run alongside weekly town markets. To the collector these stalls represent a possible Aladdin's Cave. Theses markets often run once a week and are advertised in local newspapers. I have stumbled across these events more so by luck. On the odd occasion I have found mats, usually tucked away in a plastic carrier bag or shoe box. Excited at the prospect of finding something new (well I really mean old, in good condition and going cheap!!) I run through piles of mats like juggling a pack of cards only in most instances to be disappointed. I have yet to find anything of major significance (or to brag about within this book). In the majority of cases where I have found mats nine times out of ten they have been foreign, trade or cigarette mats. My words of advice are to ask the stall holder, don't be afraid of getting your hands dirty, dig in there – you never know, you may have better luck than me.

Newspaper Adverts

I have to admit that despite all my efforts over the years I have had little success in this area. Some newspapers offer free advertising space whilst others charge per word etc. I have tried both and whilst I did receive some responses I often found that having gone to review the collection on offer 99% I either already had or were of no use to me (foreign etc). Furthermore trading on some ones door step can be awkward especially when it comes to negotiating a price.

I have seen other collectors place adverts in my local papers and later in discussion discovered that by sheer luck, good timing or whatever their efforts proved more successful than my own. I have also been approached by some collectors to asses a collection in my area on their behalf. Again these visits did not uncover anything of interest.

I would recommend that using the free adverts is still of use. People do respond, and you can judge over the phone if you think it is worth the time and effort to travel to look at the collection. Ask for any specific examples especially thick board mats or those with printers names on them.

Friends & Family

This is a great method of increasing your collection. I have constantly reminded my friends, family and work colleagues to pick up mats on their travels and holidays. This has resulted in a network of contacts that now no longer require prompting – if they are on holiday or relaxing in their local as soon as they see a beer mat they think of me. I have been handed mats from various foreign locations. I regularly receive mats advertising hotel and foreign beers, whilst I do not collect these types; I accept them gladly and pass them on to other collectors.

Printers Sample Packs

Whilst printers don't necessarily welcome collectors to visit their premises, several offer sample packs via the internet. Printer like brewers are running a business and don't have the time to show collectors around. Additionally if tours or visits were available the printer becomes responsible for the health and safety of the visitor. The sample packs tend to be provided in packs of 25 and contain a random selection of recent runs. Again the printer will not have the time to handle individual requests for specific mats.

British Pub Coaster Companies

These companies often purchase packs of mats from printers and offer the collector packs of mats. Again the selection is random and tends to be marketed towards foreign visitors as gift packs. Occasionally these companies sell packs containing a badged glass, a bar towel and a few mats. A number of these collectors' packs are numbered into series, with each series having a different selection. These gift packs can usually be found in souvenir shops and in airports.

Tipplefair

This is a regular collector's event held every 6 months in Milton Keynes, Buckinghamshire. This is a specialist event aimed specifically at collectors of Breweriana. Sellers are required to book a table space in advance. Individuals can register their interest with the organisers and will receive regular updates on planned events either by post or e-mail. I understand that these events are well attended and that there is a wide range of items being offered. Keen collectors can pay a small premium for early entry ahead of the public. Contact details are listed in the appendices section.

Junk Shops

Well, you never know your luck…These type of shops have all sorts of items for sale. As the saying goes "someone's junk is another person's treasure". These shops often obtain goods by house clearances. I have often found that you have to ask if they have any beer mats as the shop floor is usually crammed with all sorts. I have had the odd success in this area but I have found that the mats are over priced.

Antique & Collectors Fairs

These are professionally organised events often held in town halls or large indoor halls. The majority of goods for sale are antiques (trinket jewellery, furniture, retro clothing, and military goods). Many events cater for the collector and the likes of postcards, pottery, books etc are well represented. On my travels I have come across one or two stalls dedicated to Breweriana items but again the goods are often marked up to the top end of the valuations. There are many books and guides (ie: Millar's collectables) which give market valuations but always remember that you will pay more for top end goods ie; no damage, in original packaging, complete sets or matching pairs.

Beer Mat Calendar

Many breweries have traditionally produced mats to commemorate specific annual events. Look out for mats in the pubs on the following dates or periods

- St Patrick's day
- St George's day
- Halloween
- Christmas

Breweries such as Guinness and John Smith's usually issue mats to advertise annual events which they sponsor such as the Cork Jazz Festival, Six Nations rugby tournament, Galway races, Grand National etc.

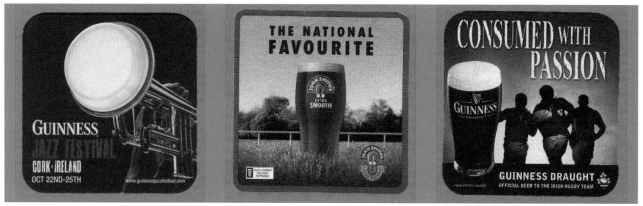

Guinness 1369 (f)   J.Smith 225 (f)   Guinness 1378 (f)

In 2006 the Black Sheep brewery issued a calendar titled "Ewe "r" a star" which themed sheep in various famous films. The calendar displayed the set of 6 mats which were released every two months.

Mats have commonly been used as:

- Postcards
- Competitions – Quiz/trivia questions
- Quotes/poetry/Crossword puzzles

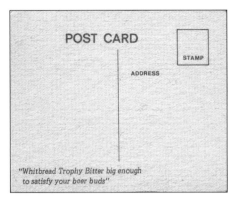

Whitbread 309 (r)

Whitbread 309 (f)

Youngers 236 (f)

Youngers 363 (f)

M. Brown 149 (f)

M. Brown 151 (f)

Robinsons 165 (f)

Robinsons 186 (f)

Maintaining your collection

Storage

Over the years I have used various methods to protect and store my collection. At first I used to display them on my bedroom wall (it's a "student" thing). The next method involved batching mats together by type – brewery/cigarette/whisky/trades etc. I would stack them into piles of about 50 and keep them grouped together with elastic bands. I would then simply keep these batches in boxes acquired from work. As my collection grew it was relegated to the attic. I cleared a space in the loft and laid down some "tongue and groove" boards to provide floor space and to carry the weight. Eventually the boxes grew as my interest increased actively trading with numerous collectors throughout the country. Following advise from other collectors I began to use clear freezer bags to either protect individual mats or batch a few mats together (possibly a series of mats).

I continued to look out for better storage facilities as I found it time consuming working my way through numerous boxes and batches whilst checking individual mats. I came across metal trays which whilst not ideal appeared more suitable than the boxes. The disadvantage of the trays was the overall weight and the fact that they could not stack and consequently took up more floor space.

My next storage facility was noticed whilst at work. Stackable plastic boxes were being used to hold spare parts for a manufacturing line. After some negotiation, I left the depot with thirteen of these boxes. On returning home I transferred all 13,000 plus mats which immediately improved the access and layout of my collection.

Several years later I came across the ideal storage box in a large DIY chain outlet. Having recognised their potential I hastily visited all their branches in the local region ending up with about 50 boxes at around £10 a time. A lot of money but this was seen as an investment.

The trays are the most suitable that I have found – the drawers slide out and the boxes are stackable. Each tray holds about 200 mats. There are also one drawer trays available which are suitable for larger mats. I have added plastic separator cards to index mark each brewery. This gives the collection a professional finish – uniform and clean. I have since added more boxes as my collection has continued to increase.

There are many other ways to store mats –

- Shoe boxes – depending on the size of your collection these boxes may prove suitable as they can be labelled and stacked for convenience

- Books/folders – I have seen several collections stored in plastic sheets or stuck into "scrap books" – again disadvantage is you can only fit a maximum number of mats per book before it's full. Sticking mats on to paper is not recommended as this may mark the mat when you come to remove it.

- Chest of drawers – this is a suitable method of storage. Mats can be stacked "up right" in rows. Downside is height and depths of drawers may restrict quantity and type of mat being stored. May need several units to house your collection.

- Visit your local record shop and ask for the boxes that compact disks are delivered in. These are ideal for most common sized mats.

Condition

Every collector would prefer to have mats in pristine condition. Alas this is a dream. My words of advice are to accept mats in any condition and look to replace them in the longer term. I generally ask the bar staff for clean copies from behind the bar rather than pinch them off the tables. Be cautious with mats that are damp as this moisture may affect other mats. I have many mats in my collection that I have picked up over time that are damaged either by light or beer stains, pin holes, cracks, tears, sellotape marks, scribbled notes etc. Some of these mats are extremely rare and I do not anticipate finding another copy. It is better to have a damaged copy than no copy at all.

Be aware that beer mats can attract woodworm. If you are storing mats in the loft check for dampness and ensure you spread the weight across the floor space or across supporting beams. The last thing you would want is several boxes of mats stacked crashing through your ceiling. Also be extra cautious of you plan to store your mats in the cellar. Every winter the news reports of over flowing rivers flooding local housing and shops. You don't want your collection sailing down the river.

I have picked up many mats that have not been in the best of condition. I find it very frustrating that some collectors have chosen to place a small sticker or label on to the mat to note the catalogue number. Whilst I have successfully removed lots of these stickers without any damage at the same time I have removed others which has either left a mark or even slightly ripped the mat. My advice to collectors who want to label mats is to either write the number in pencil, which can be easily rubbed out or to place the mat inside a plastic bag then place a label on the bag. This method has the additional benefit of protecting the mat. Suppliers (see appendices) offer a range of sealable bags in different sizes suitable to fit most mats.

Other collectors have offered various methods of recovering damaged mats including soaking the mat, however, I feel somewhat reluctant to do this as I do not wish to cause further damage to the mat. I would rather have a soiled or damaged mat in my collection than no mat at all.

Mats with small rips or tears can be artificially repaired using appropriate coloured pens to touch up the damaged area. Slightly soiled or marked mats can be improved by lightly using a rubber over the area – but don't rub too hard else you may end up causing more damage. It is best to experiment on a few spare mats first before attempting to repair your most recent prize.

Who Brewed That?

Often many mats are issued without any reference to the brewery. This makes cataloguing a difficult task. One idea to help track down the "owner" is to use an internet search engine. This may provide links to press releases or comments on web sites. Should you have little success I would suggest contacting the BBCS who between the members have extensive knowledge to help you identify the mat in question. The Society includes a comprehensive list of beers which is included within the appendices section of this book.

Dating Your Mats

Many beer mats were produced to advertise a particular product or event. Each mat represents a little piece of history. Many mats have survived over the years ending up in the care of a collector. Mats can be dated based upon certain facts that can be drawn from information on the mat such as:

In the 1930-60's many mats appeared with the printers name at the bottom. Look out for

- Quarmby (or JQH, BC/M)
- Abbot Brown (Twickenham)
- A.F. Ltd
- A J.E. Ing
- A. Pifer Ltd
- Causton London
- Corfield, Mitcham
- Daisy
- Print & Paper Ltd
- Trecise (Burton)
- Halmac. Leeds
- Hancock, Corfield & Waller Ltd
- Hancor Mitcham
- Hobsons Hull (Foreign)
- Horrocks & Co Ashton
- Nayler
- Nayprint
- N.L. & Co. Ltd
- "Novo" Series
- Maiden
- Magic Mat
- Mancunian Showcards
- Regicor (London)
- Philip & Tacey, Ltd., London
- Scottish Auto. Ptg. Co. Limited
- Woollen & Co Ltd, Sheffield

Numerous early mats were printed on the continent (usually catalogued as export issues)

- Rob Otten (Belgium, Brux, Lille)
- Hotel Printing Co., Montreal, Que
- hmT (South Africa)
- Imprime En Belgique
- Ch. Vidrequin. Papier. 171. R. Du Noyer. Bruxelles
- Louis Hecht & Fils Bruxelles
- O. Lebbe. 172. Av. Charles V Brux
- Etablissement G. Inglis. Bruxelles. D.R.P
- B. Cahen (Brux)
- Cartonnerie De Waterloo (Belgique)
- Leibenguth Strasbourg

Additionally the following lists other references often seen on early issues

- British Manufacture
- Made in England
- Printed In England
- Printed In Great Britain
- Printed In Holland
- Printed In Ireland
- Produce Of Germany.
- Made In Germany
- Foreign
- Imprime En Belgique
- Printed In Belgium
- Importe De Belgique

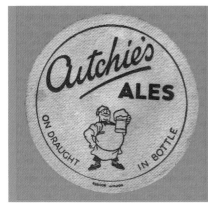
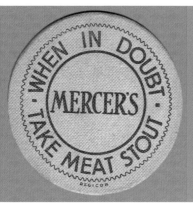

| Aitchison 2 | Duttons 4 (r) | Tennents 5 |

Regicor issues

| Aitchison 3 | George 2 | Wm Younger 4 |

Hancor Mitcham

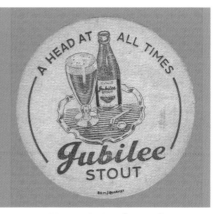

| Bernard 3 | Everards 3 | Hope & Anchor 10 |

Quarmby

| Campbell, H& K 1 | Morison 1 | Wright's 2 (f) |

Tresises

Many pre-1939 mats had a printers name on them, however having this stamp does not necessarily mean that it dates from this early period. Often a printers name combined with thick board material (3 to 4mm) and covered with evenly spaced indentations (known as a pitted surface), is usually a good clue to consider the mat to be pre-war. The board type did not change until the 1960's when thinner, smoother board was introduced. Until around 1956 it was common to find the printers name on mats. Other printer's names which have appeared on more recent issues include the likes of –

- o C.T.P. Ltd
- o Clegg Litho
- o Screenlitho
- o Scottish Automatic Printing

- o Salesprint
- o American Coaster Co
- o KP
- o Yorkshire Printers

Companies registered their Trade marks, recipes and brand names to stop other companies making fake copies or simply trying to trick customers into buying what they thought were competitor's products.

Very few breweries have maintained comprehensive records or archive material. Historians have gathered sufficient information from various sources (ex staff, brewing logs, company records etc) to determine dates. The printers themselves only hold details for limited periods either due to lack of space, time or the customer may have moved to another printer.

As a final point, please be aware that being pre-war does not necessarily mean that the mat is of greater value. Today many of the more common issues are still around in quantity and occasionally there's the odd occasion where a collector stumbles upon a supply of what up to that point was considered rare.

Display

This is a difficult one as it depends on your audience. Many collectors (and students) use mats to decorate bedroom walls. Whilst this method is certainly eye-catching it is renowned for damaging the mats. Often sellotape or drawing pins are used, both of which leave the mat damaged. I have also seen lots of mats further damaged with smoke or sun stained, both of which distorts the colours on the mat (whites shades into yellow).

Another method of display involves sheets of wood. If you plan to mount mats on a board I would suggest that the mats be placed in plastic bags and then pin the bag to the board. One thing to be wary of is theft. I have known incidents where mats displayed on boards left unattended have "disappeared" so if you intend to display in a public area check out their security arrangements beforehand.

Personally I have found that my website is the best forum to display my collection. The web allows worldwide access, little restrictions and is available online every day of the year.

The BBCS uses professional display boards. These are lightweight and the display collapses into sections which can be transported with little trouble. The overall display can be extended by adding further sections. Whilst ideal for the Society for use at meetings, these displays tend to be expensive and as such inappropriate for most collectors.

Size / Specialisation

As your collection expands you may wish to decide to downsize and possibly concentrate on only collecting a particular type of mat. This categorisation can be based on unlimited criteria:-

- UK brewery mats
- Foreign mats – ie; European or worldwide
- Particular brand or type – ie; Guinness, micro brewery or cider
- Theme – ie; sport, animals or airlines
- Date – ie; pre-war (1939), 1970-
- Regional – by county

This list could be exhaustive and is down to the individual. Having been through this exercise many years ago I chose to collect only UK brewery mats and simply gave away all my other mats to other collectors free of charge. You could consider exchanging the mats you no longer wish to collect in return for others that you have chosen to focus on.

I know many collectors or have seen adverts requesting for example, mats to do with darts, mats issued by a particular brewery between specific dates etc.

Whilst I am content with my decision to specialise I often ponder as to how many mats I would have had today if I had not given the others away. Concentrating on one theme or type may limit your scope, reducing the quantity available for you to chase so please give this serious thought before you embark on breaking up your collection.

Variations

Many breweries initially order mats in batches for immediate use in the pubs, clubs etc. This means that they do not have to worry about organising storage. Furthermore by issuing them into the field they can save additional transportation costs. Once this batch has been used, breweries simply request a reprint of similar numbers usually with the same printer. The printer should simply reuse the original artwork and printing plates ensuring colour matches etc. Occasionally the printer may choose to use a different machine or cutter resulting in either glaring changes from the original or a subtle change in colour variation. Whilst a simple re-run should be more or less be an accurate match issues such as weather conditions (too hot or cold) or a different batch of board may resulting the slightest of difference. To the keen collector these variances are of interest. The first mat printed should be strong in colour whilst towards the end it may vary slightly as the ink thins.

For a mat to be listed as a separate entry in the catalogue it must be within the guidelines ie; defined size of cut, borders, colours, text lengths etc. Those mats that are out with these guidelines are mentioned within the original catalogue entry (noted as "also found with..."). Over the years there have been many disputes from collectors seeking their new find to be accepted as a new issue rather than a variation. Some collectors are happy enough just to have one whilst others seek out the numerous variations. It is a question of personal choice.

By comparing both mats side by side occasionally other differences come to light

- Mat dimensions (width)
- Square or rounded corners
- Text size differences (length/height and letter spacing)
- Colours have changed – ie; yellow now appears as orange
- Shading – text/font
- Spacing between text and graphics
- Type of board – pitted versus smooth surface
- Material – pulp or bleached board
- Minor changes in punctuation
- Incorrect grammar
- Spelling mistakes
- Colours added or removed
- Border frame lines
- Characters – "&" and "'" are good examples
- Use of capital letters
- Letter height consistent or varied across the line

Other noticeable changes to lookout for are

- Change of address, telephone or fax numbers
- E-Mail or web site addresses
- ABV/Gravity
- List of beers – seasonal, listed in different sequence
- Competition closing dates
- Text distributed across a different number of lines

Answers can be found on page 72

Value

As I stated earlier as with any collectable item the value is in the eye of the beholder and it's a question of supply and demand. What you may be willing to pay for something is your own valuation and consequently others may disagree.

I do not intend to cover monetary values in any great detail. I do not collect mats for an investment. Yes I am willing to spend money on mats (no receipts!!) but I do not anticipate making a quick buck. Yes people do spend lots of money on purchasing mats but it should be noted that these experienced collectors recognise the rarity of the mat in question and therefore expect to pay top dollar. The problem which affects everyone (not just tegestologists) is that the seller assumes that every mat he has for sale is of similar high value. This leads to an unrealistic expectation and an air of mistrust between the seller and buyer.

I would state that probably 95% of all collections can be classified as common. The remaining 5% contains the odd mat of some value but there's a line to be drawn between buying one individual mat or the whole lot.

The BBCS runs auctions at both local and the annual National collectors meetings. I am often surprised to see many mats reach unbelievable prices for something that is either more common than the bidders know, or the fact that I possibly picked my copy up for free at the time. I recall numerous occasions where I have given the unsuccessful bidder my spare copy for nothing. This gesture often has its rewards long term as the bidder may return the favour one day.

I do not expect to ever have every known UK Brewery mat in my collection. For one there are simply not enough original copies to go around let alone being able to afford them all. This is a realistic expectation and with this in mind I simply aim to keep pace with the new issues as they are released and to pick up the odd mat off my lists.

Insurance

Most companies will offer insurance cover for fine art and antiques but I have been unsuccessful in obtaining insurance cover for my beer mat collection. Sizeable collections present the collector with a unique set of risk exposures and insurance considerations. There are several points of cover that are worthy of note and some are listed below:

- Cover against fire and theft
- Cover for collections on display or stored in multiple locations
- Full Transit Cover
- Automatic Cover for New Acquisitions
- Access to specialist loss adjustors
- Basis of Settlement Agreed Value

In a conversation with a DJ who owns a massive record collection he advised me that he would need to insure each one individually as if they were rare works of art or paintings. Based upon these facts I have found it uneconomical to have my collection insured. I have always thought that, dare I say, should something happen to my collection I would simply start again.

The British Beer Mat Collectors Society

The British Beer Mat Collectors Society was formed by Chris Walsh in 1960. His objective was to meet with other collectors in order to share his hobby with like minded collectors whilst increasing public awareness and adding to his collection. An advert in the Exchange and Mart magazine brought about sufficient response that inspired Chris to form the BBCS. A regular sixteen page newsletter was distributed to members. The magazine provided information on new mats and Society arranged events. As membership increased, a committee was formed and the Society published a set of rules and objectives.

In order to publicise the Society, the membership appointed a publicity officer. The aim of this position was to ensure that the Society and hobby was promoted in order to gain new members.

In the 1960's television personalities Morecombe & Wise were appointed as Society Presidents. Apparently both were avid collectors and are known to have welcomed and exchanged with members at theatre stage doors. Mackeson have issued a number of mats advertising Morecombe & Wise shows on the reverse.

| 212 (f) | 212 (r) | 214 (r) | 216 (r) |
| 218 (r) | 220(r) | 221 (r) | 222 (r) |

The monthly newsletter soon outgrew its roots and was changed to a magazine format. The magazine included information on new mats, society meetings, members' adverts etc. Good relations were formed with breweries and liaison schemes were agreed whereby a locally appointed member would regularly obtain supplies of the latest mats from the brewery. These issues were then listed in the magazine and available upon request from the liaison officer. This arrangement meant that the breweries were not inundated with individual requests for mats. Members were advised not to write to these breweries involved in this scheme.

Today this scheme is still in place however generally managed through the Society shop. Mats obtained on behalf of the Society are managed centrally and offered through the magazine.

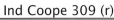

Ind Coope 309 (r)

Ind Coope 327 (r)

Ind Coope 342 (r)

Ind Coope 249 (r)

Watney's 98 (r)

Enamel Badge

Button Badge

ARE YOU A TEGESTOLOGIST?

If you collect beermats why not join the British Beermat Collectors Society?

- Monthly newsletter containing details of newly issued mats
- Meetings held throughout the country for collectors to swop mats
- Annual International Exchange Meeting held over 2 days in aid of charity
- Catalogues available listing mats in various categories
- Collections purchased to provide a good range of mats for BBCS auctions
- Overseas Liaison Service for foreign members unable to attend meetings
- Society Shop for newly issued mats
- Joint events held with other brewery related Societies

Founded 1960

Society Magazine front cover 1987–88

Subscriptions

The annual fee for membership is recommended by the Hon. Treasurer during his report on the Society finances during the Annual General Meeting. Any change requires approval from the members and is put to a vote.

As a member you will receive and have access to the following benefits:

- Monthly newsletter – articles and listings of the latest new issues reported to the museum curator. Details to Society organised events (Monthly meetings held throughout the country). Reports on meetings, list of new members. Opportunity to buy mats through the Society shop. Members can place adverts looking to trade mats.

- Society membership mat

- Membership list

- As a member you can attend the AGM and can vote on Society matters

Catalogues

The Society offers catalogues for sale which describes in MS word format textual descriptions of the mats. These are available to members on compact disc. Catalogues are available for the following categories' –

o British Brewery	o Gin
o Foreign Beers in the UK	o Hotel
o Brandy	o Plastic
o Cider UK	o Pretend
o Cider Foreign	o Rum
o Camra	o Shows TT
o Festivals	o Society
o Food	o Tandem
o Forces	o Vodka

Mats are catalogued, where possible in chronological date order. Members can check their mats against these lists. Where known the mats are also dated. The descriptions are abbreviated to help reduce the overall volume of text. As new mats are reported in the monthly magazine they are allocated the next sequential number and appended to the listings.

Abbreviations used in catalogue descriptions –

- Cir   Circular
- Sq   Square
- Oct   Octagonal
- Rect   Rectangle
- Hex   Hexagonal
- Tri   Triangular
- Ov   Oval
- Loz   Lozenge
- Shpd   Shaped
- Blk   Black
- Wt   White
- Gy   Grey
- Gn   Green
- Blu   Blue
- Bn   Brown
- Bu   Buff
- Gld   Gold
- Gn   Green
- Pk   Pink
- Pur   Purple
- Or   Orange
- Rd   Red

- Sil   Silver
- Tor   Turquoise
- PS   Pitted Surface
- SS   Smooth Surface
- BB   Bleached board
- WP   Wood pulp
- 1/0   Printed on one side only
- 1/1   Printed same on both sides
- 1/2   Printed (different) on both sides
- BA   Brewers address
- BN   Brewers name
- BNA   Brewers name & address
- LD   Line drawing
- PN   Printers name
- DW   Drink warning
- TM   Trade mark
- Reg   Regicor
- Q   Quarmby
- JOH   Quarmby
- T   Trecises
- Han   Hancor

This is an example;

Abbey Ales Ltd, The Abbey Brewery, 2 Landsdown Road, Bath

Commenced brewing in 1997.

1.   [ ]   Arch. 1/1. Cm/Gld/Wt/Blk on Mar. (Gld border, 2 Gld frame lines) TM (abbey in oval) Abbey Ales Bellringer ABV 4.2% Brewed in Bath   2000
www.abbeyales.co.uk

Catalogue no

1/1 – same design both sides

Arch shaped

Colours –

Cm – cream
Gld – gold
Wt – white
Blk – black
Mar – maroon

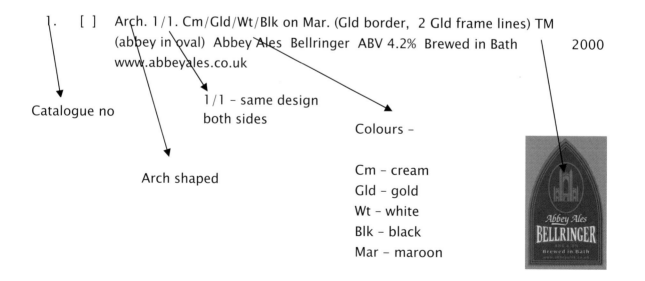

International Collectors Meeting

Each year the Society arranges a two day collectors meeting. These meetings are usually sponsored by a brewery and a proportion of the monies raised is split between a local and a selected national charity. In the months leading up to the event, the appointed organiser approaches breweries to obtain supplies of mats (and items of Breweriana) that are then made available at the meeting. The event is open to non-members as well as the general public, except during the AGM which is open to members only. The meeting has a fixed format which includes the auction of mats throughout both days. The climax of the event is the auction of the Collectors Top 10 mats. These mats have been individually selected from Society stock (acquired from the purchase of collections from either retiring members or from approaches from the general public). The committee collectively agrees the purchase price of collections offered for sale.

The meeting caters for all collectors as stalls are split into various categories (UK brewery, foreign beers, cider, misc etc). Additional tables offer items of Breweriana and mats from Society stock for sale. Other collectors Societies are invited to attend. Furthermore the nominated charity is usually represented.

Breweries are requested to submit mats into the "Mat / series of the year". These mats are openly displayed and members are asked to vote for their top three in each category. Once the competition closes the voting slips are counted and the winning entries announced. The Society then arranges to present a shield and framed certificate to the winning brewery.

Once all monies are collected and expenses paid out the Committee decides on the charity allocation. The presentation is usually arranged around a Society meeting with the press being invited along for publicity.

The National meeting is usually well attended with members travelling from all around the world. Having signed in to the meeting, you can purchase mats either from the stalls or from the auction. Furthermore many collectors exchange mats with other collectors as well as picking up from piles of free mats provided by members (known as a "drop-out").

During the 1990's the Society appointed Ronald McGill (Amos from ITV's Emmerdale Farm program) and Bob Holness (from the television quiz show "Blockbusters") as Hon Presidents. During their "term in office" both attended the National meetings which attracted television, radio and press coverage.

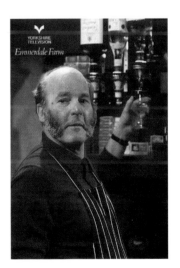

The event is publicised locally well in advance. The sponsoring brewery usually commissions a number of mats to advertise the event. These are normally distributed into local pubs and clubs to advertise the meeting in advance resulting in new members or people offering collections for sale.

Committee - AGM/Constitution

The Society is managed by a small number of members who form a "virtual committee". A number of positions are noted as Honorary –

- Chair person
- Treasurer
- Editor

There are six other positions that form the committee and duties are assigned on a voluntary basis. Posts are advertised in advance of the AGM and any position that receives a number of applicants is voted upon by the members. Posts can only be held for a maximum of three years unless no one comes forward.

The Committee is responsible for managing the Society matters and membership is governed by a constitution. This document lists the various rules and regulation in relation to administration and conduct. Any committee meeting must have a quorum of at least five members. The committee may also invite individuals to manage various tasks.

The Society is a non-profit making organisation and is not VAT registered. Prior to the AGM the financial records are independently audited.

Museum

Over the years the Society has built up its own collection of mats known as the museum. The Society owns a number of collections boasting numerous mats, many of which are noted to be the only known copy in existence. The collections are the property of the members and are stored by a number of volunteering members. These mats are not offered for sale thus ensuring that no one individual benefits from having these ultra-rare mats. Whilst these museums represent a major asset the value is not reported on the annual accounts. This is simply due to the fact that it would be too difficult to put any value against the collection as the value cannot be assessed (supply versus demand).

Shop

The role of "mat organiser" is key to obtaining mats on behalf of the Society. This is a demanding role and takes up a lot of time. Having developed a network of contacts at breweries and printers the aim is to secure sufficient quantities to supply the members. When a supply is received priority is given to Society arranged meetings (as advertised in the monthly newsletter). This is to encourage members to attend their local meetings. Remaining stocks are then offered to members through the shop. Any offers are listed in the magazine and supply is subject to demand.

Misprints & Errors

Occasionally a mat is found to contain a spelling error. Missed by the printer or the brewery before release these mats are often discovered by the eagle eyed collector. There are numerous examples noted over the years, here are a few examples –

This Eldridge Pope issue contained a spelling mistake.

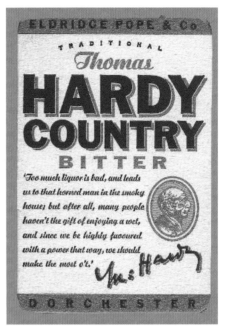

183 (f) (Liqour)   185 (f) (Liquor)

Harveys issued the this mat with a spelling mistake on the reverse

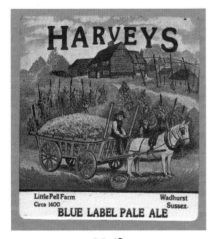

11 (f)   11(r) (Susssex)   13 (r) (Sussex)

Tennent's issued two sets of 6 mats with a common reverse which listed the delivery characteristics. Unfortunately they did not notice on the initial release that the temperature was incorrect – it read 6 degrees instead of 4.

269 (r)

276 (r)

In 1961 Ushers of Wiltshire issued a mat to advertise their Goldcrest brand. On the initial mat the wrong bird was illustrated.

14

15

Ind Coope's first series of 15 mats titled "story of beer" was released with two numbers nine's.

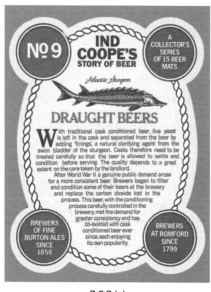
303(r)

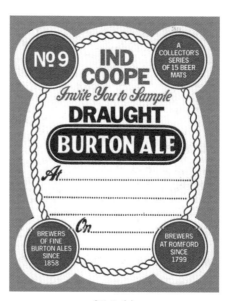
311 (r)

Ingenious Ideas

Every now and then someone comes along with an idea that is remarkably clever and in the advertising world this may give the seller that competitive edge over the competition.

In 1992, the Parish Brewery issued a set of 5 mats on a thick cardboard material. Each mat displayed a different brew. The gravity of the beer was represented by the time on the church clock ie; 10:44 meant a gravity of 1044. A further mat was issued in 1994 advertising Radio Leicester with the radio frequency 104.9 being represented on the clock face as 10:49.

5

6

7

8

9

11

These two mats issued by Banks are designed to give the impression that one mat looks larger than the other when placed side by side. The mats are in fact the same size.

270 (f)

271 (f)

This is not a misprint – it is designed to question if you may have had too much to drink.

Bruce 54 (f)

Front & Rev of 30-32

In 1965 Ushers of Edinburgh issued this mat which used invisible ink. When the front centre panel was moistened it would reveal one of three messages. This message disappeared as the mat dried out. The exposed message revealed either "major prize", "free entry" or "hard luck try again".

Beer Goggles

In 2000 Guinness issued a set of six competition mats to identify the Hurling player. The player's faces were distorted on the mat however when a pint glass was placed on the mat the image was reflected on the glass to help the customer recognise the player in question.

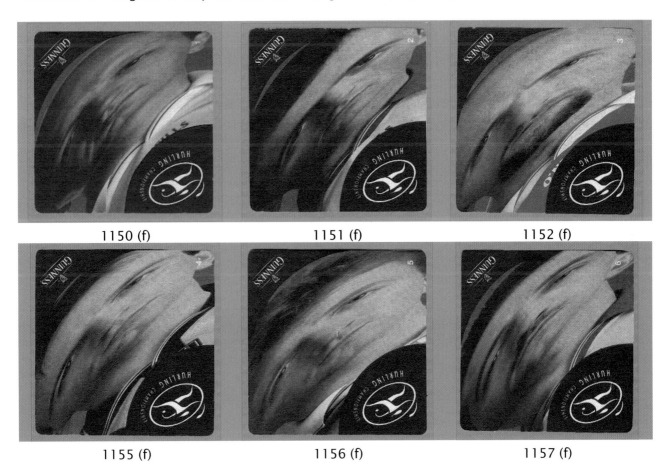

| 1150 (f) | 1151 (f) | 1152 (f) |
| 1155 (f) | 1156 (f) | 1157 (f) |

Sand Mats

An early example of ingenious advertising is of three mats issued by William Younger of Edinburgh in 1939. These mats are known as "sand mats" as sealed within a transparent area is a small quantity of sand. The concept of the mat is for the sand to replicate flowing beer as it passes between the scenes portrayed on both sides. In the first example below, the front side shows the bar maid pouring beer from a barrel into the glass. As the mat is turned over, the sand flows in the opposite direction appearing as if the man is drinking the beer from the glass.

These mats are very rare and very few exist with the sand intact. Whilst probably impractical for use on pub tables, many collectors have viewed these as show cards and not as beer mats.

14 (f)   14 (r)

495 (f)   495 (r)

522 (f)   522 (r)

The Birth of the Micro brewery

During the 1960-1970's the industry was dominated by what became known as the Big 6 brewers. The six where - Bass Charington, Courage, Whitbread, Allied (Ansells, Ind Coope, Tetley Walker), Watneys, Scottish and Newcastle.

The brewing industry has seen the demise of many regional brewers being taken over or merging with others. The objective was to increase the pub estate into which they could sell their mass produced national brands. In the short term this led to redundancies and breweries being closed with beer production being transferred to the regional brewery which usually had spare brewing capacity. Management were more interested in keeping costs down at the expense of flavour. The result of these takeovers is that many famous names and beers were axed. The effect to the local pub goer is usually broken promises, less choice, bland beers, a hike in prices and the loss of a local brand.

National brands -

- Youngers - Tartan Keg
- Watneys - Red Barrel, Manns, Truman
- Allied - Skol Lager, Tetleys, Ind Coope Double Diamond
- Whitbread - Mackeson, Forest Brown, Tankard
- Bass - Charrington, Brew XI, Worthington
- Courage - Tavern

Watneys 145 (f)

Ind Coope 47

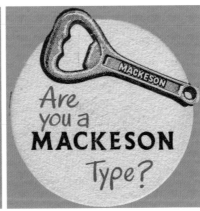

Mackeson 27

Skol 53

In the 1970's, backed by the Campaign for Real Ale, Micro breweries started to appear. Their objective was to compete in their local market and to offer high quality beer whilst offering drinkers a wider choice and consistent quality. Unfortunately the big players' dominance in the tied pub estates squeezed many micros out of business unable to find regular outlets to take their beers. In the 80's the Government passed regulations to reduce the stranglehold that the brewers had by lowering the number of pubs any one brewer can own. Additionally legislation was passed (The Beer Orders) to ensure the tied houses sold a guest beer. Whilst this opened the door for the micros, the big brewers worked around this by setting up exchange deals and alliances with other brewers.

The impact of legislation meant that breweries sold off less profitable (uneconomic outlets) or rural pubs allowing them to hold on to the pubs in city centres. In recent years the big brewers have concentrated more on pub estates than on brewing. This investment in pub estates gave rise to the themed pubs. Predominantly aimed at the student market place numerous pub chains soon appeared. These pubs were stripped of any history or local character and replaced, in my opinion, with cheap gimmicks. Pubs were furnished in replica themed memorabilia; Interiors were refurbished with cosy quiet areas being demolished to open up large potentially noisy, smoke filled areas.

These chains did initially prove successful but in the long run customers began to see through the whole themed pub concept. However the latest initiative which is proving popular are "Sports Bars" where pubs are fitted out with a number of large plasma television screens and decorated with various types of sports memorabilia. These pubs draw large crowds especially when big events are being televised.

Many big brewers made large investments out with brewing and have expanded into the leisure market having purchased restaurants, hotel chains and holiday complex centres. This has allowed small and independently owned brewers to compete equally in a large market space. Rather than brew beer many companies have transformed into pub owning chains (Pub Co).

These are examples of mats issued by:

- Matthew Brown – issued in 1985 protesting against S&N's unwelcome take-over bid.
- S&N – set of mats issued in 1988 in protest of Fosters of Australia's approach.

Brown 121

S&N 87

S&N 88

S&N 89

Whilst the big brewers produced beer in high volumes a number chose to have a presence in the real ale market and opened small brew houses. These were in direct competition to the micro brewers.

Today there are a number of supporting bodies and schemes designed to help the independents and micro breweries.

- Campaign for Real Ale (CAMRA) – this is an independent consumer organisation aimed at promoting real ale.
- Small Independent Brewers Association – this is a body formed by brewers with the objective of providing support within the group.
- Cask Marque – this is an initiative, backed by the brewing industry with the aim of improving the quality of cask beer. Pubs are inspected for excellence in Cellarmanship and good beer keeping.

Other initiatives introduced over the last few years have included "The drink awareness campaign". This body is aimed at promoting responsible drinking. Several brewers have subscribed to this and promote the group and message on beer mats.

Micro breweries continue to go from strength to strength with the numbers increasing month by month. The loss of major industries throughout the UK has changed peoples life with many deciding on a career change by taking up brewing, investing their redundancy money in brewing equipment and small premises. Many have lasted the pace, content to develop and maintain a local customer base whilst other collapsed due to poor quality or simply not selling enough beer to remain afloat. There are several consultancy firms around today providing start up advise and support to potential brewers.

Some micro brewers have faced the problem of becoming too successful too quickly, thus unable to keep pace with demand or struggling to maintain plant to supply the market. Beer kegs are expensive commodities and are often the target of theft. The loss or non-return of these kegs means that the brewer has to either invest in purchasing more or spending time tracking down his stock within the field.

In recent years a number of beer distribution companies have started up with the aim to provide a carrier service for small breweries or independents. These companies haul beer supplies across the UK supplying regular outlets and beer festivals. This service is of great value to brewers as it means they can spend more time managing their brewery rather than being out on the road.

Many micros' have only limited advertising budget and prefer to invest this in the likes of pump clips to go with the kegs rather than on beer mats. From those who have chosen to have mats printed it can be stated that they have made the beer mat an art form with some excellent colourful eye catching graphics usually accompanied with a clever brand names for their brews.

Afan 1	All Nations 1	Ayrshire 1
Beacon 1 (f)	Bird In Hand 1	Blackawton 4 (f)
Bruces 21	Butcombe 1 (f)	Fighting Cocks 1
Fox & Hounds 1	Hilden 1	Hoskins 2 (f)

Litchborough 1	Ma Pardoe's 1 (f)	Miners Arms 1 (f)
Oakhill Brewery 1 (f)	Penhros 2	Pollards 5
Ringwood 1 (f)	Saxon Cross 1	Selby 1
Studley 3	Three Tuns 3	Victoria 1

Blue Anchor 1	Dock Brewing 1 (f)	Dog & Parrot 1 (f)
Frog & Parrot 1 (f)	Fox & Newt 1 (f)	Lass-O-Gowrie 1
Gate Ale 1 (f)	Guiseley Gyle 2 (f)	Hall Cross 1 (f)
Oxford Bakery 1 (f)	Rose & Crown 1 (f)	Thompsons 1 (f)

Guinness

Guinness is famous for its advertising campaigns. They are legendry. Backed up with vast budgets specialist consultants rather than frontline advertising agencies are employed to promote the "Black stuff".

In 1927 S.H. Benson was the first company to be employed to commission poster campaigns. Over a period of 35 years artist John Gilroy created over 100 press and poster adverts for Guinness. Gilroy left Bensons in the 1940's but continued to work on a freelance basis into the 1960's. His designs are still being used by Guinness marketing all over the world. Memorable iconic designs include the toucan and the zoo animals with slogans such as "my goodness my Guinness". Other long standing campaigns included "Guinness is good for you" which eventually had to be withdrawn as advertising bodies questioned the statement.

Guinness merchandise has become very collectable. The Guinness website offers an online store which stocks a wide range of goods (from clothing to barware). In recent years Guinness has entered new territories previously un-captured markets other than by local breweries. The demise of capitalism has opened the door for Guinness to enter the likes of Russia and the Ukraine. Trading barriers have been removed allowing access to Japan and other Asian countries. Even countries surrounded in religious beliefs are seeing Guinness brands appearing for the first time.

| Israel | Japan | Slovakia | Russia |

In the UK, the Guinness brand is a household name, promoted as a way of life. Expensive television adverts usually run during the breaks in sporting events have captured the imagination of both drinkers and non-drinkers. Guinness has the most listed entries within the BBCS UK Brewery catalogue.

1318–1337

Withdrawn

Occasionally mistakes or errors are made which go unnoticed in the editing or proofing stage and consequently are released unknowingly. Furthermore the context of the advertisement may offend people and complaints are raised with the standards authorities. These complaints can relate to false claims, sexual discrimination or be deemed offensive. A few examples are listed below all of which following complaints that were upheld forced the brewery to withdraw the mats (either by destroying the remaining stock or recalling what was left from the pubs). These mats then become much sought after by the collector.

Sexism

The example quoted here comes from a set of four mats issued by Castlemaine in the UK. People complained about the double entendre implied in the text.

False Claims

In 2002 Gales issued two sets of mats claiming that beer was healthy as it contained a high concentration of vitamins. Following complaints the Trading Standards Authority forced the brewery to withdraw the claims.

40 (f)

40 (r)

45 (f)

46 (f)

Offensive

In 1988, Hartley's brewery issued a mat advertising their brand Xplosive Bitter. Unfortunately they chose to link the beer with the term "Unexploded bomb". People took offence to the graphics and the mat was hastily withdrawn.

20 (f)

20 (r)

Copyright

Over the years there have been several new products launched into the market which have infringed copyright or patents owned by others. The Bass Red Triangle trademark was Britain's first registered trademark dating back to 1876. Other notable trademarks include Guinness name and Harp trademark. More often when noticed the larger corporate usually threatens court action against the small offender and they are forced to re-brand.

A recent incident involved the brand St Peters where the St Peters brewery challenged the Houston brewery. The Houston brewery ended up renaming their product "St Peter's Well". Other known disputes include John Smith using the brand name "Classic" which infringed Castella's copyright. Another dispute involved the use of the "Huntsman" trade mark both used by Eldridge Pope & Tetley.

Eldridge Pope 4

Tetley 6

Permission

Several years ago Webster and Wilsons Ltd brewery produced two sets of 24 mats featuring questions titled "Brain Beaters" which featured Carol Vorderman. It is understood that Carol objected to her name being used in the promotion and the brewery was forced to destroy all copies. A few sets were rescued and ended up in the hands of keen collectors.

These two mats issued by an agency on behalf of Newcastle Breweries (catalogue no 189). Unfortunately, the brewery for some reason did not like the initial release and subsequently withdrew the mat and had the reverse re-designed.

 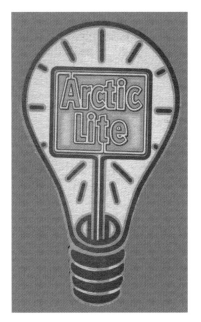 

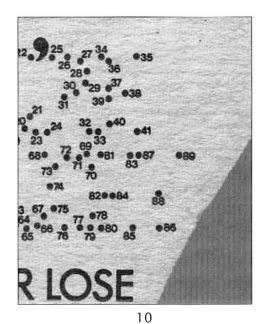

10

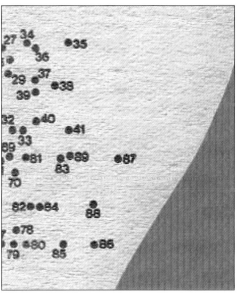

11

In 1978 Allied Breweries issued this light bulb shaped mat (cat no 10) with an offer on the reverse. On joining the dots together there were two possible messages portrayed – "you're a winner" or "you're unlucky". The initial mat issued (number 10) into the pubs had the dot position in the wrong place (on the unlucky mat – 89 is furthest dot on right). This was reissued in 1979 (cat no 11) to correct the error (87 now furthest right).

In the news

Beer mat that knows when it is refill time

Two German students have created a device that will stop beer lovers having to get out of their seats for a refill – sensor chips inside the beer mat alert bartenders that a customer needs a new drink. The "smart" beer mat, created by Matthias Hahnen and Robert Doerr from Saarland University in Saarbruecken, southwest Germany, can sense when a glass is nearly empty, sending an alert to a central computer behind the bar so waiters know there are thirsty customers. The plastic beer mat had sensor chips, which measured the weight of the glass, embedded inside. When the weight of the glass drops to a certain level, the sensor chips detect that it is close to empty and alerts the bartender via a radio signal. "You could have hundreds of beer glasses in the bar and the beer mat would, for example, tell the bartender, 'table 14 needs a refill", say the creators. Unlike the usual cardboard beer mats, the invention is made out of plastic, which means it does not absorb water. They could also be used as a "voting system" during karaoke competitions: patrons could raise their glass if they liked a singer, or flip it over if they did not. (Source: BBC News website)

Beer mat flipping 'perfected'

Engineering experts have come up with a way of improving one of the favourite pub games enjoyed by British drinkers – beer mat flipping. Through a series of experiments, engineers have come up with a new design that gives an added edge to the traditional pastime of flipping a mat up from the edge of a table and catching it mid-air. Ian Johnston, an aerodynamic expert at the Open University, and Hazel Lucas, who is doing a masters in engineering at Oxford University, spent two months working on the project.

To help them, they constructed a special machine designed to simulate the action of a person flipping a mat from below. Mr Johnston said: "The first part of the research, which was particularly enjoyable, involved going to a canalside pub and experimenting with the different beer mats. "We found the mats behaved differently, mainly according to their shape but also their size and how you balance them on the table." Further tests found the key to the perfect flip was to have as much of the mat over the table's edge as possible to be able to strike it near the centre. Mr Johnston and Ms Lucas experimented with 35 designs before settling on one they considered the best. The final design, called the Aeromat, looks much like any square beer mat but uses an arched-shape piece of cardboard, two-thirds of its length. The last third is made from foam, lighter than the cardboard, allowing more than half the mat to balance over the table's edge. It also has a plastic V-shaped wing on either side designed to keep it level in flight and close to the flipper, making it easier to catch.

David Hodge, marketing manager for cider Strongbow, which commissioned the research, said: "This is a breakthrough for the legion of pub sportsmen who have been flipping with equipment unchanged in decades." Bulmers, makers of Strongbow, have sent consignments of the new Aeromats to student bars at Manchester University, Nottingham University and University College London to test them before it considers whether to distribute them elsewhere. (Source: BBCS News website)

Beer mats ads target potential priests

Staring through the bottom of an empty glass in a bar might not seem like the obvious moment to consider becoming a priest, but it could become the norm under a novel recruitment scheme hatched by the British Catholic Church. Alarmed at a recent decline in priest numbers, the country's Catholic hierarchy is to print advertisements seeking new priests on beer mats, the cardboard squares used in pubs and bars to rest drinks on. (Source: ABC Online news)

Beer & Sandwich boards

As plans are announced to engage disaffected voters by trialling online ballots, a more low-tech tactic is spilling over into the mainstream – beer-mats. When the Home Office launched a campaign in Dec 2003 to alert students to the dangers of crime, it knew exactly where to publish its "awareness-raising" information – on beer-mats.

The Good2BeSecure campaign, fronted by David Dickinson, whose BBC One show Bargain Hunt has become a cult hit among the young , offers students "top tips" on how to protect their property from burglars. Beer-mats have been distributed to student pubs around the country, warning: "Don't let them bag your booty! Nearly half of all burglaries are through an open door or window."

This isn't the first time that those in authority have tried to communicate with young people via the medium of the beer-mat. The beer-mat in particular appears to have become a point of contact – for everything from facts and figures about health and crime to encouraging teens and twenty-something's to engage in politics.

New Labour's first venture into propaganda-by-beer-mat was largely a gimmick. At the Labour Party conference in September 2000, party officials distributed a beer-mat ridiculing then Tory leader William Hague's boast that he once drank 14 pints. Waving the beer-mat in the air, Deputy Prime Minister John Prescott claimed the choice for Britain was between "Tory froth and Labour delivery". Journalist Simon Hoggart noted that, "In the past parties had manifestos; in 1997 they brought in pledge cards; now we have beer-mats."

In the run-up to the general election of 2001, Labour MP Andrew Smith took the beer-mat approach to politics a stage further. Smith's young activists gave out beer-mats in local pubs, encouraging students to "vote Labour". East Northamptonshire Council used beer mats to try to drum up interest in the local elections. "XXXX – it's not a dirty word. Vote 1st May 2003," said the 5,000 mats distributed to pubs, hotels and off-licences. (Source: BBC News website)

Health awareness

The beer-mat has been used to raise awareness about health issues among the young. In Wales, the Health Promotion Division made a beer-mat for distribution in pubs and clubs last year, advising young men to think seriously about safe sex. "Protect your prop forward!" was the witty motto, with a picture of a man in his underpants stretching a condom. (One landlord banned them from his pub on the grounds that a photograph of bulging underwear might offend patrons.) Macmillan Cancer Relief also issued beer-mats with eye-catching photos. The mats showed close-up shots of a man's chest and a woman's cleavage, with the words "CHECK 'EM OUT". It is only when you flip the mat over that you realise it is an attempt to alert people to the symptoms of lung cancer. (Source: BBC news website)

Mats on test

A beer mat designed to detect date-rape drugs has been withdrawn from the market after it failed several laboratory tests. Proofies, produced by SureScreen Diagnostics of Derby, are advertised as a safe and reliable way to protect against date-rape drugs. But tests at St George's Hospital in London for BBC Radio's PM programme showed the product failed to detect benzo-diazapines, a drug used in date-rape cases, in several cases. The beer mat has a strip on it which is meant to change colour if the drink is contaminated. The company was withdrawing the product from the market while further trials were completed. (ref: BBC news website)

Jolie collects beer mats

Superstar actress ANGELINA JOLIE has started collecting beer mats as a reminder of her time spent living in rural England. The TOMB RAIDER beauty has lived in Fulmer, Buckinghamshire, for the past two years and loves the various designs of beer mats because they are "so British". Jolie told drinkers at The Black Bull pub of her collection. An onlooker tells British newspaper The Sun, "She made everyone laugh by flipping a beer mat and saying she had a big collection."

Accident 'victims' on beer mats

Images of road accident injuries are to feature on beer mats as part of a new safety campaign in Lancashire. The faces of two students from Blackpool and Fylde College appear on the mats. They show the students looking healthy on one side, but the reverse reveals the injuries car crashes can cause.

Police plan to distribute them among pubs and clubs across the county to encourage young people to wear seatbelts. Posters showing similar images will also be used. Lancashire Police aims to note the number of teenagers they spot wearing seat belts and write to congratulate them. The campaign is part of the Department of Transport's road safety 'Think' campaign. (Source: BBC News website).

It's a fact

Beer mat psychology...

Did you know that when feeling anxious, people are more likely to tear a beer mat into small strips, while the more comfortable and outgoing individual will try to flip the beer mat and catch it. However most people will just read the advert on the beer mat!

Personality profile...

A survey conducted by Gaymer's concluded that a persons character can be identified by the way they fiddle with beer mats. One third of those questions are "flippers" (place the mat on the edge of the table, flip them into the air and catch them). A quarter are labelled "shredders" (folding the mats before tearing them to pieces). Twelve percent are scribblers (using the mats to scribble notes or telephone numbers on). Sculptors account for eleven percent (make origami figures from a pile of mats). The remainder fall into collectors or those who enjoy throwing them across the pub floor.

Did you know?

- Beer mats can absorb moisture up to 300% of their own weight

- It would take 16,170 standard sized mats laid end to end to cover one mile.

- Mat Hand (yes, that's his name) is noted as having flipped and caught 112 mats on May 9th 2001 at Waterstone's bookshop gallery in Nottingham. It took him 4 hours and 129 attempts before he broke his previous attempt of 111.

- Mr David Armitage holds the unusual title of having stuffed the greatest number of beer mats into the mouth and held in the teeth. Using standard sized beer mats he achieved the grand total of 77 – Don't try this at home folks!!

- In 1970 beer mats were used as cheques during the Irish bank strike

- Due to the risk of someone throwing a mat across the pub and striking someone in the face, for health and safety reasons mats are no longer produced with square corners.

- Checkout this online game involving the use of beer mats

www.essexnightclubs.com/games/beermat.html

Europe

- On the European continent, mats are used to keep a tally of the number of drinks bought by the customer. Each time you order a drink a notch is marked onto your beer mat and then at the end of the evening, the bar staff will add up your notches and you can settle your account all in one go. This is a very trusting system that nobody seems to abuse.
- The European Parliament ruled that no beer mat should be used twice, something about it being unhygienic. So if, when you take a seat at a table in a pub in Europe, you find a beer mat there that's had one side peeled off, has got some doodlings on it and a complete stranger's phone number, or indeed any other signs of previous use, then you will know that that the pub you are in is breaking the law.

Biggest & Smallest

- The record for the largest UK Brewery mat is owned by Theakston's. In 1994 they commissioned a small run of oval one sided shaped mats (cat no 52) that measures 102cm x 78.8cm.
- The honour of the smallest mat belongs to the Steampacket Brewery. Catalogue no 30 issued in 1995 measures just 18mm.

Steampacket 30 (f)

Answers to spot the difference (page 40)

- Warwick's (top) – the woman on the right has a pocket on her apron

- Kitchen (middle) – the colour of the grapes on the two mats are different (red on one, green on the other)

- Wm Youngers (bottom) – whilst there are minor differences in the size of the text the main difference is the " ' " character in Younger's (one is rounded the other square)

A Decade of New Issues

I recall reading a newspaper article a number of years ago reporting that there was imminent legislation being passed through the European Community Parliament that would be the death of the beer mat. It stated that for public health reasons, mats could only be used on pub tables for one night only then had to be replaced as they could spread germs etc. Given the costs to print mats it was quoted that they would likely disappear over time. As a collector this was alarming news. Whilst some legislation has been introduced I am happy to report that the use of beer mats as a point of sale article is still very much alive.

Having maintained the UK Brewery catalogue for a number of years, I for one know from the volume of typing (well, cut & paste) required each month that it would appear the number of new issues being reported monthly is on the increase year upon year. Putting this theory to the test I undertook an exercise to walk through all the Society magazines from the last 10 years (Jan 96 – Dec 05) and count up the number of new issues reported over this period. I then entered the numbers into a spreadsheet and the findings are plotted below.

With respect to the years with high numbers they tended to include large series such as Firkin mats, World Cup series mats from Harp & Beamish and pub & clubs outlets from the likes of Guinness and Beamish. So over the 10 years there have been a total of 4948 UK brewery mats listed (6421 if you include export issues).

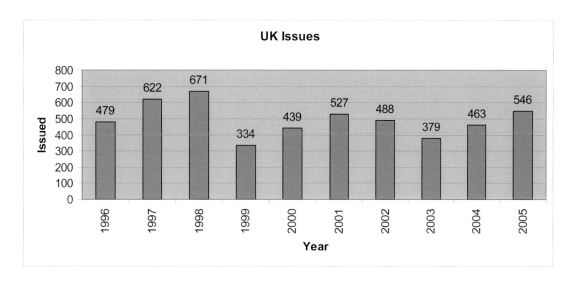

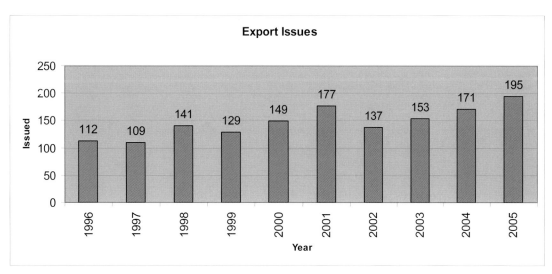

Beer mat Translations

Nation	Country	Translation
	America	Coaster
	Czechosovakia	Pivni tacek
	Denmark	Olbrikker
	France	Sous Bock
	Germany	Bierdeckel
	Holland	Bierviltje
	Italy	Sottobicchieri di birra
	Poland	Podstawki
	Russia	Podstavka dlia piva
	Slovakia	Podpivnik
	Spain	Posavasos
	Sweden	Ett olunderlagg

Appendices

Identity parade

Having difficulty cataloguing that mat? Don't known which brewery it belongs to? Use these lists to help identify the brewery

Details on mat	Brewery
ld of acorn & oak leaves	Barnsley Brewery Co. Ltd
ld of harp	Arthur Guinness Son & Co Ltd
ld of hind's head	Whitbread & Co Ltd
head & shoulders of huntsman holding glass	Tetley Hotels
ld of large Y	George Younger & Son Ltd
ld of magnet	John Smith's Tadcaster Brewery Co Ltd
ld of man (Dr Johnson) on shield	Courage & Barclay Ltd
ld of seahorse	Belhaven Breweries Ltd
ld of swallow	Vaux & Associated Breweries Ltd
ld of toby jug on triangle	Bass plc
ld of toby jug	Charrington
12 Bore	Free Traders
1880 Club	Eldridge Pope & Co Ltd
2 pint take home containers	Courage plc
2 pint take home containers	John Smith's Tadcaster Brewery Co Ltd
A. B. C. Best Bitter	Aylesbury Brewery Co. Ltd.
Abbey Original Bitter	Shepherd Neame Ltd
Abbot Ale	Greene King & Sons Ltd
Ace Draught Lager	Charles Wells Ltd
Ace of Clubs	Northern Clubs Federation Brewery Ltd
Air	Mash & Air Brewery
Aitchie	Aitchison (John) & Co
AKA Extra Strong Lager	Courage plc
Alpine Lager	Samuel Smith Old Brewery (Tadcaster)
Alton Bitter	Courage & Barclay Ltd
Amboss Lager	Hydes Anvil Brewery
Anglian Strong Bitter	Norwich Brewery
ARC Premium Lager	Bass plc
Arctic Light	Allied Breweries (UK) Ltd
Arctic Lite	Allied Breweries (UK) Ltd
Are you going for a pint?	Smithwick & Sons Ltd
Ask here for a cask beer	Tollemache & Cobbold Breweries Ltd
Auld Soxx	Surrey Free Inns
Badger	Hall & Woodhouse Ltd
Banbury Ales	Hunt, Edmunds & Co Ltd.
Barbican	Bass plc
Barbican	Mitchells & Butlers (M&B) Ltd
Barclay Stout	Courage & Barclay Ltd
Beaver Export Lager Beer	Greenall Whitley Export
Bedford Ales	Charles Wells Export
Bedford Brewery Company	Charles Wells Export

Details on mat	Brewery
Beer... naturally	Bass plc
Beer Pitcher	Scottish & Newcastle Breweries
Benfro	Pembrokeshire Own Ales
Bentley's Yorkshire Bitter	Whitbread East Pennines
Bergman's Lager	The Wrexham Lager Beer Co Ltd
Best Mild XXXX	Bass plc
Best Scotch	Castle Eden (Whitbread)
Big Pint	Arthur Guinness Son & Co Ltd
Birds Of Martin Mere	Whitbread West Pennines
Bishop's Castle Ales	Three Tuns Brewery
Bishop's Tipple	Ushers Wiltshire Brewery Ltd
BL	Carling Export
Black	Carling Export
black & white	Arthur Guinness Son & Co Ltd
Black Dove	J & R Tennent Ltd
Bleu de Brasserie	Allied Breweries (UK) Ltd
Blezards Traditional Bitter	New Fermor Arms
Blue Can	Threlfalls Chesters Brewery Co. Ltd
Bobby Ale	R. W. Randall
Boddies	Boddingtons Breweries Ltd
Boxer Ales	Randalls Vautier Ltd.,
Breaker Malt Liquor	J & R Tennent Ltd
Brenin Bitter	Crown Buckley Breweries
Brew Ten	Bass plc
Brew XI	Bass plc
Brew 70	Castle Eden (Whitbread)
Brewed In Lancashire	Whitbread West Pennines
Brewed In Yorkshire	Whitbread East Pennines
Brewer's Own	Ely Brewery Co. Ltd
Brewers Own	Rhymney & Crosswells Breweries Ltd
Brewmaster	Flowers Breweries Ltd
Briggan	Allied Breweries (UK) Ltd
Brock Lager	Hall & Woodhouse Ltd
Brookside Brewery	Gartside's (Brookside) Brewery Ltd
Brubecker	Bass plc
Buccaneer	Burtonwood Brewery Co (Forshaws) Ltd
Buchanan	Northern Clubs Federation Brewery Ltd
Bulldog Pale Ale	Courage plc
Bulldog Strong Ale	Courage plc
Bulls Eye Brown Ale	Greenall Whitley & Co Ltd
Burns	Drybrough & Co Ltd
Burton Ale	Ind Coope & Allsopp Ltd
BYB	Whitbread East Pennines
'C' Ale	Groves & Whitnall Ltd
C & S	Catterall & Swarbricks Brewery Ltd
Caffrey's	Bass plc
Calders	Archibald Arrol & Sons

Details on mat	Brewery
Campbell's	Whitbread Campbells
Caraca Caine Beer	Bass plc
Caseys	Shepherd Neame Ltd
Cask Ales	Whitbread & Co Ltd
Castle Keep	Castle Eden (Whitbread)
Celebration Ale	Beamish & Crawford Ltd
Celebration ELA Ale	Taylor Walker (Ind Coope) Ltd
Celtic Smooth	St. Austell Brewery Co Ltd
Champion	Greenall Whitley & Co Ltd
Charter Ale	Castle Eden (Whitbread)
Charter Original	College Ales
Chelt Ales	Cheltenham & Hereford Breweries Ltd
Chester Brown	Greenall Whitley Export
Chester Gold	Greenall Whitley Export
Chester Golden Ale	Greenall Whitley Export
Chesters	Chesters (Whitbread)
City	Norman & Pring Ltd
Club Better Beers	Lancashire Clubs Federation Brewery
Club Brewery Beers	South Wales & Monmouthshire Clubs
Club I•P•A•	Northants & Leicestershire Clubs
Club Royal Brown Ale	Northants & Leicestershire Clubs
Clubs Brewery	Northants & Leicestershire Clubs
Clubs Brewery Beers	Yorkshire Clubs Brewery Ltd
Colne Spring Ale	Benskins Watford Brewery
Coopers Beers	Allied Breweries (UK) Ltd
Cornish	Devenish & Co Ltd
Cotswold	Stroud Brewery Co Ltd
Coulsons	Steel, Coulson & Co Ltd
Country Brew	T. D. Ridley & Sons
Craftsman Traditional Premium Ale	D. Thwaites & Co Ltd
Crawford's Golden Ale	Beamish & Crawford Ltd
Crest Lager	Courage Breweries Ltd
Crest Premium	Courage Breweries Ltd
Crown	Charrington
Cwrw Mon	Gwynedd Brewers Ltd
Cynful	R. W. Randall
Dalkeith Ales	McLennan & Urquhart Ltd
Danny Brown	D. Thwaites & Co Ltd
Daredevil	Everards Ltd
Dasher Downing's Draught	Fox & Hounds (Woody Woodwards)
DD	Ind Coope & Allsopp Ltd
Deakin's	Mansfield Brewery Co. Ltd
Dempsey's	Hall & Woodhouse Ltd
Devil's Kiss	Allied Breweries Export
Diat Steam Bitter	Devenish & Co Ltd
Diamond Bitter	Ind Coope & Allsopp Ltd
Diamond Heavy	Alloa Brewery Co Ltd

Details on mat	Brewery
Dobbins	West Coast Brewing Co Ltd.
"Doctor" Brown Ale	Barclay, Perkins & Co Ltd
Don Jon	Tennant Bros Ltd
Doolish Manx Stout	Isle Of Man Breweries
Dorchester Bitter	Eldridge Pope & Co Ltd
double Chelt	Cheltenham & Hereford Breweries Ltd
Double Dan	Daniell & Sons
Double Diamond	Ind Coope & Allsopp Ltd
Double Maxim	Vaux & Associated Breweries Ltd
Double Star	Charles Wells Ltd
Douglas	S & N, Gordon & Douglas
Dowie's	Scottish & Newcastle Breweries
Downham Ales	Castle Hotel
Dragon's Back	Castle Eden Brewery
Draught Burton Ale	Ind Coope & Allsopp Ltd
Draughtpak	Scottish & Newcastle Breweries
Dreadnought	Thornley-Kelsey Ltd
Duchy Bitter	St. Austell Brewery Co Ltd
Duddingston	Robert Deuchar Ltd
E	Museum Brewing Co
Eagle	Charles Wells Ltd
Eagle Bitter	Charles Wells Ltd
Eagle Brewery	Leicester Brewing & Malting Co Ltd
Edelbrau Diat Pils	J. W. Lees & Co. (Brewers) Ltd
Edelbrau Lager	J. W. Lees & Co. (Brewers) Ltd
Eiger Lite Lager	Samuel Smith Old Brewery (Tadcaster)
E.S.B.	Fuller Smith & Turner Ltd
Executive Bitter/Mild	Peter Walker (Warrington) Ltd
Executive Lager	Northern Clubs Federation Brewery Ltd
Extinct Species	North Country Breweries Ltd
Extra Light	Bass plc
Falmouth Bitter	Devenish & Co Ltd
Falstaff Scotch	Joshua Tetley & Sons Ltd
Farmer Brown	Style & Winch Ltd
Federation	Northern Clubs Federation Brewery Ltd
Festival Export Ale	Greenall Whitley & Co Ltd
Fine Diploma Ales	Henry Tomlinson Ltd
Finian's	Celtic Brews
Finnegans	T. D. Ridley & Sons
Five Hides Bitter	Inn Off The Green
Flagon Four	Whitbread & Co Ltd
Forest Brown	Whitbread & Co Ltd
Forshaws '67' Stout	Burtonwood Brewery Co (Forshaws) Ltd
Frisk	Vaux & Associated Breweries Ltd
Full Brew	Courage Barclay & Simonds Ltd
Full Brew Bitter	Courage plc
Ganz	Grand Metropolitan Plc

Details on mat	Brewery
George's Best	Ansells Cambrian
Get Into It	Smithwick & Sons Ltd
Gillespie's Malt Stout	Scottish & Newcastle Breweries
Gilmour's Bitter	Tetley Gilmour
Gloster Stout	Cheltenham & Hereford Breweries Ltd
Gobbledy Goose	Hall & Woodhouse Ltd
Gold Bier Premium Lager	J & R Tennent Ltd
Gold Cross Lager	S. Allsopp & Sons Ltd
Gold Label Barley Wine	Whitbread & Co Ltd
Goldrush	J.W. Cameron & Co Ltd
Gold Strike	Watney Combe Reid & Co. Ltd.
Golden Mead Ale	Hope & Anchor Breweries Ltd
Gordon	S & N, Gordon & Douglas
Gray's	Licensed Wholesale Consortium
Great Cock-Up	Boddingtons Breweries Ltd
Great Western Bitter	Crown Brewery Co Ltd
Great Western Bitter	South Wales & Monmouthshire Clubs
Green Label Ale	Samuel Webster & Sons Ltd
Greenmantle Ale	Broughton Ales Ltd
Green Top Pale Ale	Eldridge Pope & Co Ltd
Gretel Pilsner Lager	Red Tower Lager Brewery
Guards Ale	Bentley & Shaw Ltd
Guards Ale	Hammonds United Breweries Ltd
Guards Heavy	J & R Tennent Ltd
Halloweeness	Guinness Export
Hampshire Bitter	Whitbread Wessex
Hector's Bitter	Hall & Woodhouse Ltd
Heldenbrau Lager Beer	Whitbread & Co Ltd
Hemeling Lite Lager	Mitchells & Butlers (M&B) Ltd
Highway	Elgood & Sons Ltd
Hobnobs Original	Castle Eden (Whitbread)
Hoffmans Lager	Cherry's Breweries Ltd
Holtenbrau Lager	Joseph Holt Ltd
Hop Pit	Inn Off The Green
Hunter Bitter	Scottish & Newcastle Breweries
Huntsman	Eldridge Pope & Co Ltd
Husky Lager	Tollemache & Cobbold Breweries Ltd
Idea Lager Beer	Smithwick & Sons Ltd
Imperial Ale	Joshua Tetley & Sons Ltd
Ind Coope Sales	Allied Breweries (UK) Ltd
In All Kinds Of Weather	Vaux & Associated Breweries Ltd
Irish Drinks	Smithwick & Sons Ltd
J. B. A. Premium	J. B. Almond Ltd
J. D. Dry Hop Bitter	Devenish & Co Ltd
J. K. Lager	King & Barnes Ltd.,
Jacob's Lager	Archibald Arrol & Sons
James Ernest Bitter	Steampacket Inn

Details on mat	Brewery
James Forshaws Bitter	Burtonwood Brewery Co (Forshaws) Ltd
Jersey Brewery	Ann Street Brewery Co Ltd
Jet Stout	Guinness Export
John Bull Bitter	Ind Coope Export
John Bull Bitter	Ind Coope Romford Brewery Co Ltd
John Martin's Special	Courage, John Martin
John Peel	Workington Brewery Co. Ltd
John Peel Special Bitter	Matthew Brown & Co Ltd
John Who?	Courage, John Martin
JPS	J P Simpkiss Breweries Ltd
Jubilee	Hope & Anchor Breweries Ltd
Kaliber	Arthur Guinness Son & Co Ltd
Kellerbrau	Charles Wells Ltd
Keller Brau Lager	Charles Wells Ltd
Kellys Lager	Northern Clubs Federation Brewery Ltd
Keoghan's Ale	Northern Clubs Federation Brewery Ltd
Kestrel	William Younger & Co Ltd
Kilkenny Irish Beer	Smithwick & Sons Ltd
Killian's Irish Red	G. K. Lett Export
Killian's Red	G. K. Lett Export
Kimberley	Hardys & Hansons Ltd
King Pin Bitter	Ansells Brewery Ltd
Kings Ale	Matthew Brown & Co Ltd
König Lager	Eldridge Pope & Co Ltd
Krone Lager	Howcrofts Brewery Ltd.
Lagalime	Ruddle & Co Ltd
Lambton's	Vaux & Associated Breweries Ltd
Lancer	The Harp Lager Company
Landorf	Arthur Guinness Son & Co Ltd
LBM	Leicester Brewing & Malting Co Ltd
LCL Pils	Northern Clubs Federation Brewery Ltd
Lion Ales	Matthew Brown & Co Ltd
Lion Bitter	Matthew Brown & Co Ltd
Lion Lager	Matthew Brown & Co Ltd
Little Chelt	Cheltenham & Hereford Breweries Ltd
Lloyds	John Thompson Inn & Brewery
Lochside	James Deuchar Ltd
Long Life	Ind Coope & Allsopp Ltd
Low and no Alcohol	Whitbread West Pennines
Mac's	McMullen & Sons Ltd
Mainwaring Bitter	Saxon Cross Brewery
Manor Ales	Rochdale & Manor Brewery Ltd
Manx Cooil Lager	Okell & Son Ltd
Marksman Lager	Mansfield Brewery
Martin's Pale Ale	Courage, John Martin
Mary Ann	Ann Street Brewery Co Ltd
Masterbrew Red Label	Licensed Wholesale Consortium

Details on mat	Brewery
Matty's Light	Matthew Brown & Co Ltd
Maxim Light	Vaux & Associated Breweries Ltd
Mayflower Ale	Plymouth Breweries Ltd
McFarland	Murphy Export
Medallion Lager	Northern Clubs Federation Brewery Ltd
Mild 'N' Mix	Fuller Smith & Turner Ltd
Milk Maid Stout	John Smith's Tadcaster Brewery Co Ltd
Milk Maid Stout	Warwick and Richardson Ltd.
Milligan's Mist	Ushers Wiltshire Brewery Ltd
Mojo	Bass plc
Mr Toby's Carving Room	Charrington
Munchen Lagerbier	Scottish & Newcastle Breweries
M Y (intertwined)	Scottish & Newcastle Breweries
New Inns Bitter	Ansells Brewery Ltd
NewQuay Steam	Devenish & Co Ltd
Norseman Lager	Vaux & Associated Breweries Ltd
Norstein Lager	Wadworth & Co Ltd
Northampton Draught	Manns Northampton Brewing Co
North Brink Porter	Elgood & Sons Ltd
Northumbrian Smooth	Northern Clubs Federation Brewery Ltd
Oakwell Famous Ales	Barnsley Brewery Co. Ltd
O•B	Octagon Brewery Ltd
OB	Oldham Brewery Co Ltd
Offilers' Ales	Museum Brewing Co
Old Baily Strong Bitter	Mansfield Brewery Co. Ltd
Old Chester Ale	Greenall Whitley & Co Ltd
Old Shilling Bitter	Boddingtons Breweries Ltd
Old Thumper	Ringwood Export
Our Guarantee	J & R Tennent Ltd
Outside Inn	Vaux & Associated Breweries Ltd
Paradise Bitter	Bird In Hand
Parsons	Drink-Link
PB	Plymouth Breweries Ltd
Phoenix	Cherry's Breweries Ltd
Pick 'Em For Cash	Whitbread & Co. Ltd
Pils On Draught	Scottish & Newcastle Breweries
pint of the unusual	S & N, T & J Bernard Inns
Piper	United Caledonian Breweries Ltd
Piper Best Scotch	Bass plc
Plympton Brewery	Furgusons Brewery
Poacher Bitter	Flowers (Whitbread)
Poker Alice Premium Beer	Bass plc
Polar	Greene King & Sons Ltd
Pommies Revenge	Goose Eye Brewery
Pompey Royal	Whitbread Wessex
Pony Ales	Guernsey Brewery Co (1920) Ltd
Post A Pal A Pint	Joshua Tetley & Sons Ltd

Details on mat	Brewery
Praed's	Campbell Praed & Co. Ltd
Premium Diamond Lager	Joseph Holt Ltd
Prohibition	Devenish & Co Ltd
Pure Genius	Guinness Export
Radio Kent	Fremlins (Whitbread)
Raeburn's Best	Scottish & Newcastle Breweries
Red Cap Pale Ale	United Caledonian Breweries Ltd
Red Dawn	Castle Eden Brewery
Redeye	Mansfield Brewery Co. Ltd
Red Rose	Groves & Whitnall Ltd
Red Rose Stout	Greenall Whitley & Co Ltd
Red Shed	Dentons Brewery
Reverend James	Crown Buckley Breweries
Rheingold Lager	Oldham Brewery Co Ltd
Riding	Mansfield Brewery Co. Ltd
Rocky Pils	Scottish & Newcastle Breweries
Romford Brewery Company	Ind Coope Romford Brewery Co Ltd
Royal Oak	Eldridge Pope & Co Ltd
Royal Old English Ale	Strong & Co Of Romsey Ltd
Royal Stag	Paine Export
Royal Toby	Charrington United Breweries Ltd
Royal Wessex Bitter	Devenish & Co Ltd
Rupert Tetlow	Northern Clubs Federation Brewery Ltd
Rye Lager	Pig Brewery
S & P Best Bitter	Norwich Brewery
Sable Stout	J W Green & Sons Ltd
Sabre Lager	Everards Ltd
Saga Draught Pils	Scottish & Newcastle Breweries
St. Christopher	Allied Breweries (UK) Ltd
St. Edmund Ale	Greene King & Sons Ltd
St. James's Gate	Arthur Guinness Son & Co Ltd
Same again	Crown Brewery Co Ltd
Samson	Vaux & Associated Breweries Ltd
Satzenbrau	The Harp Lager Company
Saxon Lager	Young & Co's Brewery Ltd
Scorpion	Vaux & Associated Breweries Ltd
Shandy Pilsner	Bass plc
Ski Lager	Rhymney & Crosswells Breweries Ltd
Slalom D	Matthew Brown & Co Ltd
Slalom Lager	Matthew Brown & Co Ltd
Slalom Lager	Workington Brewery Co. Ltd
Somerset Best Bitter	Hardington Brewery
Somerset Special	Hardington Brewery
Springfield Bitter	Mitchells & Butlers
Spyway Bitter	Poole Brewery Ltd
Stag Bitter	Watney Combe Reid & Co. Ltd.
Stag Brewery (Antler)	Watney Combe Reid & Co. Ltd.

Details on mat	Brewery
Stag Lager	Watney Combe Reid & Co. Ltd.
Starkeg	Starkey, Knight & Ford
Star Light	Watney Combe Reid & Co. Ltd.
Steam Bitter	Devenish & Co Ltd
Steiger	Arthur Guinness Son & Co Ltd
Stein	D. Thwaites & Co Ltd
Steinbock	Shepherd Neame
Steingold Export Draught Lager	McMullen & Sons Ltd
Stein Lager	Phipps Northampton Brewery Ltd
Stingo No. 10	Phipps Northampton Brewery Ltd
Stocks	Hall Cross (Stocks Brewery)
Stonehenge	Chainmaker Beer Company
Straight 8	Watney Combe Reid & Co. Ltd.
Strettons Ale Trail	Shropshire Brewers
Strongarm	J.W. Cameron & Co Ltd
Strong Country Bitter	Whitbread Wessex
Stud Extra	Devenish & Co Ltd
Stud Lite	J.W. Cameron & Co Ltd
Summit Stout	Peter Walker (Warrington) Ltd
Sunbright Ale	Thornley-Kelsey Ltd
Super Draught	Ind Coope & Allsopp Ltd
Super Storm	Thwaites Export
Swallow Hotels	Vaux & Associated Breweries Ltd
Swing Inn	Allied Breweries (UK) Ltd
T	J & R Tennent Ltd
Take drinks home	Courage Barclay & Simonds Ltd
Tankard Bitter	Courage Breweries Ltd
Tartan Special	William Younger & Co Ltd
Tavern	H & G Simonds Ltd
Tavern Draught	Courage Breweries Ltd
Test Brew	Allied Breweries (UK) Ltd
The Brewery Stone Staffs	Joule & Sons Ltd
The House Of Massey	Museum Brewing Co
Time beer	Smithwick & Sons Ltd
Timothy Chudley	Gibbs Mew & Co Ltd
Tivoli	Rhymney & Crosswells Breweries Ltd
TK	Thornley-Kelsey Ltd
Toby	Charrington and Co Ltd
Toby	Charrington United Breweries Ltd
Toby Ale	Hoare & Co Ltd
Toby Bitter	Bass plc
Toby Bitter	Charrington
Toby Grill	Charrington
Toby Inns	Charrington
Toby Inns & Taverns	Charrington United Breweries Ltd
Toby Lager	Charrington
Toby Light	Bass plc

Details on mat	Brewery
Toby Light	Charrington
Toby Milk Stout	Charrington and Co Ltd
Top Hat	Burtonwood Brewery Co (Forshaws) Ltd
Tower Ales	Tadcaster Tower Brewery Co Ltd
Tower Export Strength Stout	Beamish & Crawford Ltd
Town Ales	Bentley & Shaw Ltd
Town Royal	Bentley & Shaw Ltd
Traditional Hand Pulled Ales	Bass plc
Treble Gold	Allied Breweries (UK) Ltd
Trelawny's Pride	St. Austell Brewery Co Ltd
Trent Brewery Ltd	Allied Breweries Export
Trident Hotels	Charrington United Breweries Ltd
Triple A	Allied Breweries (UK) Ltd
Triple Crown Bitter	Manns Northampton Brewing Co
Triple Crown Bitter	Ushers Wiltshire Brewery Ltd
Trophy Best Bitter	Whitbread East Pennines
Trophy Best Bitter	Whitbread & Co. Ltd
Tulip Brand De Luxe Lager	J. W. Lees & Co. (Brewers) Ltd
United Clubs Brewery	South Wales & Monmouthshire United
United Pompey Ales	Portsmouth & Brighton United
Vale of Neath Ales	Evan, Evans, Bevan Ltd
VB	R. W. Randall
Viking Lager	Devenish & Co Ltd
Vitamin Milk Stout	Hope & Anchor Breweries Ltd
WANTED	J & R Tennent Ltd
Wappy	Ainley (John) & Sons Ltd
Warwick Brown Ale	Thornley-Kelsey Ltd
W • B • Co	Wellow Brewery Co
Welsh Bitter	Whitbread Wales
Wem Ale	The Shrewsbury & Wem Brewery Co Ltd
Wem Best Bitter	The Shrewsbury & Wem Brewery Co Ltd
West Country Ale	Cheltenham & Hereford Breweries Ltd
West Country Pale Ale	Whitbread Wessex
Westerham Ales	Bushell, Watkins & Smith Ltd
Wexford Irish Cream Ale	Greene King Export
White Rose	J. Hey & Co. Ltd.
William & Mary Pale Ale	Devenish & Co Ltd
Wilmot's	Godson, Freeman & Wilmot,
Witnness	Arthur Guinness Son & Co Ltd
Worth Brewery	Commercial Brewing Co. Ltd
XD Premium Lager	Carling
Yellow Label	Samuel Smith Old Brewery (Tadcaster)
Yorkshire League Bitter	Whitbread East Pennines
Zodiac Mystic Brews	Bateman (George) & Sons Ltd

Collectors Societies

British Beer mat Collectors Society (BBCS)

The Secretary
69 Dunnington Avenue
Kidderminster
DY10 2YT

Web: www.britishbeermats.org.uk

America

American Breweriana
P.O. Box 11157
Colorado 81001-0157
USA

Web: www.americanbreweriana.org

Check out the "coasters corner" page

Germany

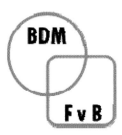

BDM/FVB
c/o Reinfried Stark
Kirschenweg 11
D-90556 Cadolzburg
Germany

Brewery History Society

Jeff Sechiari
Manor Side East
Mill Lane
Byfleet
Surrey
KT14 7RS

Web: www.breweryhistory.com

The Labologists Society

Peter Standen
16 Bognor Drive
Herne Bay
Kent
CT6 8QP

Web: www.labology.org.uk

British Brewery Playing Cards Society

Mike Johnson
65 Chandlers
Orton Brambles
Peterborough
PE 2 5YW

Web: www.bbpcs.co.uk

The Campaign for Real Ale

230 Hatfield Road
St. Albans
Herts
AL1 4LW

Web: www.camra.org.uk

Guinness Collectors Club

Web: www.guinntiques.com

Scottish Brewing Archives

University of Glasgow
13 Thurso Street
Glasgow
G11 6PE

Web: www.archives.gla.ac.uk

Beer Inn Print

Paul Travis
Long High Top
Heptonstall
Hebden Bridge
West Yorkshire
HX7 7PF

BEER-INN PRINT.co.uk
For anyone with an interest in beer

Web: www.beerinnprint.co.uk

Subscribe to "The New Imbiber" a bi-monthly magazine on UK's latest breweries and their beers.

Plastic bags

RJH Plastics
Unit 86,
Plume Street Ind Estate,
Aston,
Birmingham,
B6 7RT

GL5 – (4.5" x 4.5") or GL7 – (5.5" X 5.5") self sealing/plain bags (1,000 Per box)

Tipplefair

Peter Ballantyne,
50 Chatsworth,
Great Holm,
MK8 9BD

Web: www.tipples.net

Beery Bits & Bobs

Items for sale include T shirts, ties, lapel badges, bottle labels and beer towels all
related to the world of (mainly British) beer and breweries.

Web: www.breweriana.co.uk

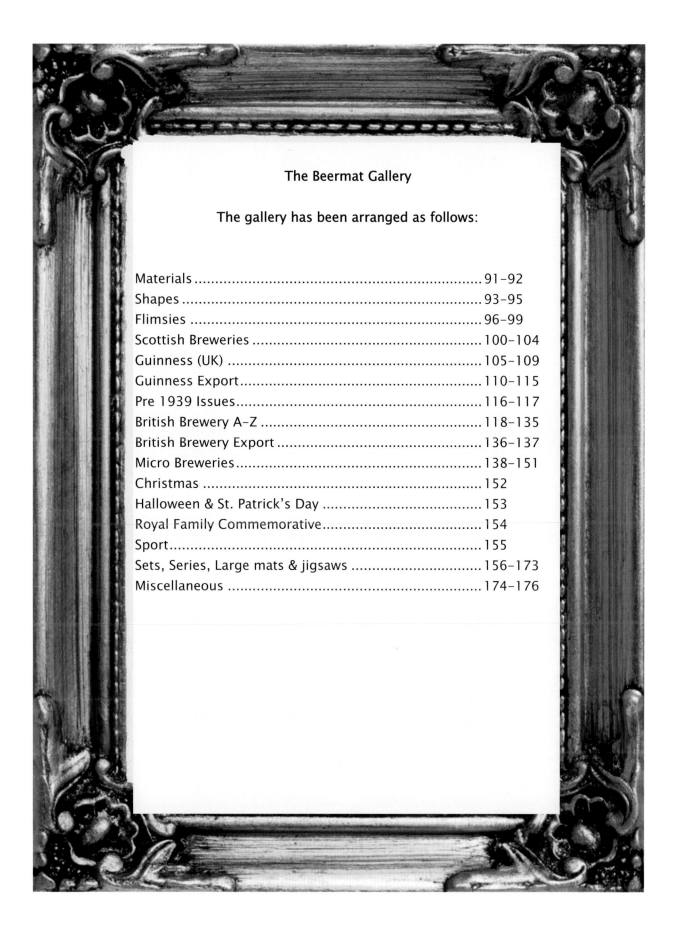

The Beermat Gallery

The gallery has been arranged as follows:

Bass Exp 61	Bruces 2	Cobbold 3
Grunhalle 61	Guinness	Hunts 12
McEwans	Murphy 84	RCH 3
Shows (unlisted)	Six Bells 1	Tennents 140
Tennents 221	Whitbread Exp 60	Whitbread Campbells 14

Materials (Pliadek)

Robert Deuchar 4	Robert Deuchar 7	Robert Deuchar 8
Hull 57	Mansfield 23	Melbourne 10

Materials (thin card)

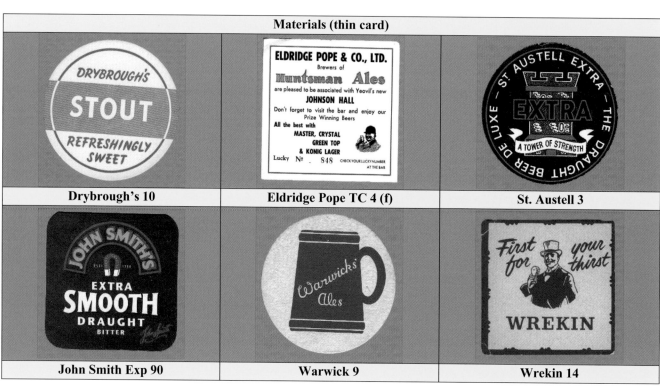

Drybrough's 10	Eldridge Pope TC 4 (f)	St. Austell 3
John Smith Exp 90	Warwick 9	Wrekin 14

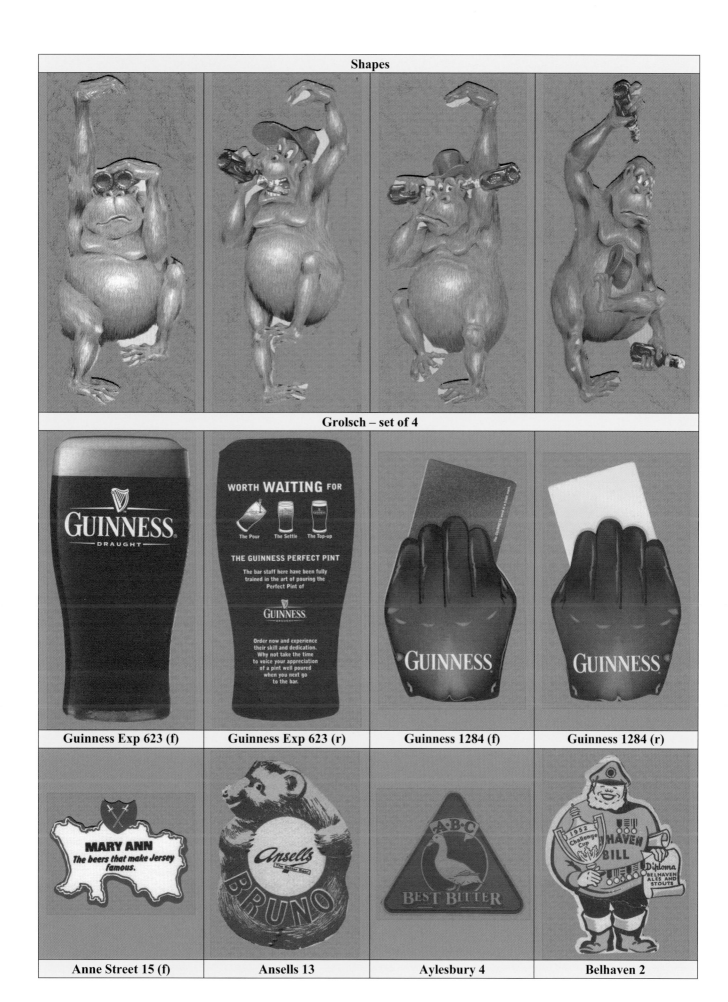

Shapes			
Grolsch – set of 4			
Guinness Exp 623 (f)	Guinness Exp 623 (r)	Guinness 1284 (f)	Guinness 1284 (r)
Anne Street 15 (f)	Ansells 13	Aylesbury 4	Belhaven 2

93

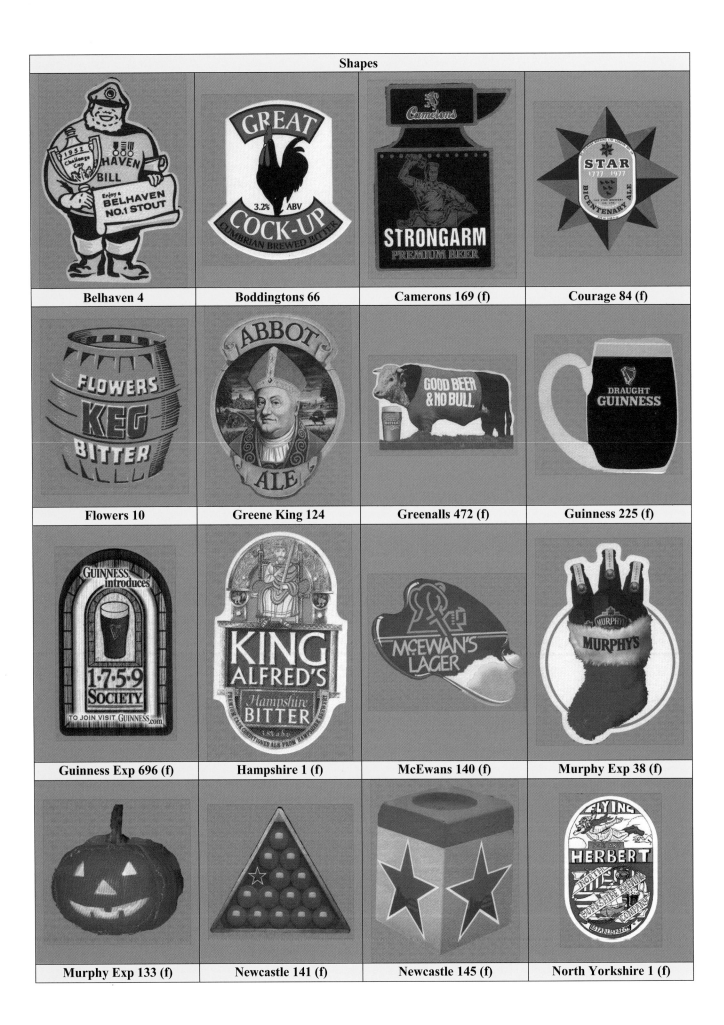

Belhaven 4	Boddingtons 66	Camerons 169 (f)	Courage 84 (f)
Flowers 10	Greene King 124	Greenalls 472 (f)	Guinness 225 (f)
Guinness Exp 696 (f)	Hampshire 1 (f)	McEwans 140 (f)	Murphy Exp 38 (f)
Murphy Exp 133 (f)	Newcastle 141 (f)	Newcastle 145 (f)	North Yorkshire 1 (f)

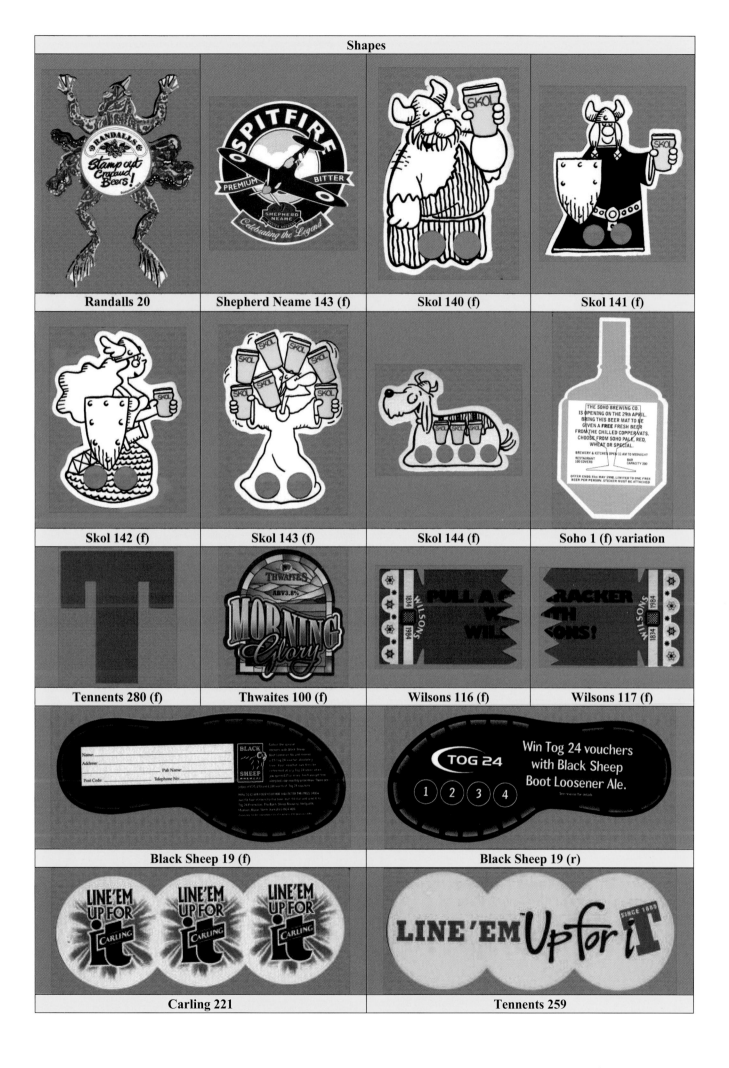

Randalls 20	Shepherd Neame 143 (f)	Skol 140 (f)	Skol 141 (f)
Skol 142 (f)	Skol 143 (f)	Skol 144 (f)	Soho 1 (f) variation
Tennents 280 (f)	Thwaites 100 (f)	Wilsons 116 (f)	Wilsons 117 (f)

Black Sheep 19 (f)	Black Sheep 19 (r)

Carling 221	Tennents 259

Anne Street 9	Banks 187	Barnsley 37	Bass 256
Bass 386	Beamish 27	Brown Hotel 2	Carling Hotel 6
Caledonian 22	Castle Eden 2	Castle Eden 3	Cathedral 1
Chelsea 1	Dempsey Exp 1	Drybrough - Hotel 144	Eldridge Pope
Freedom 2	Greenalls 429	Greenalls 443	Guinness 45

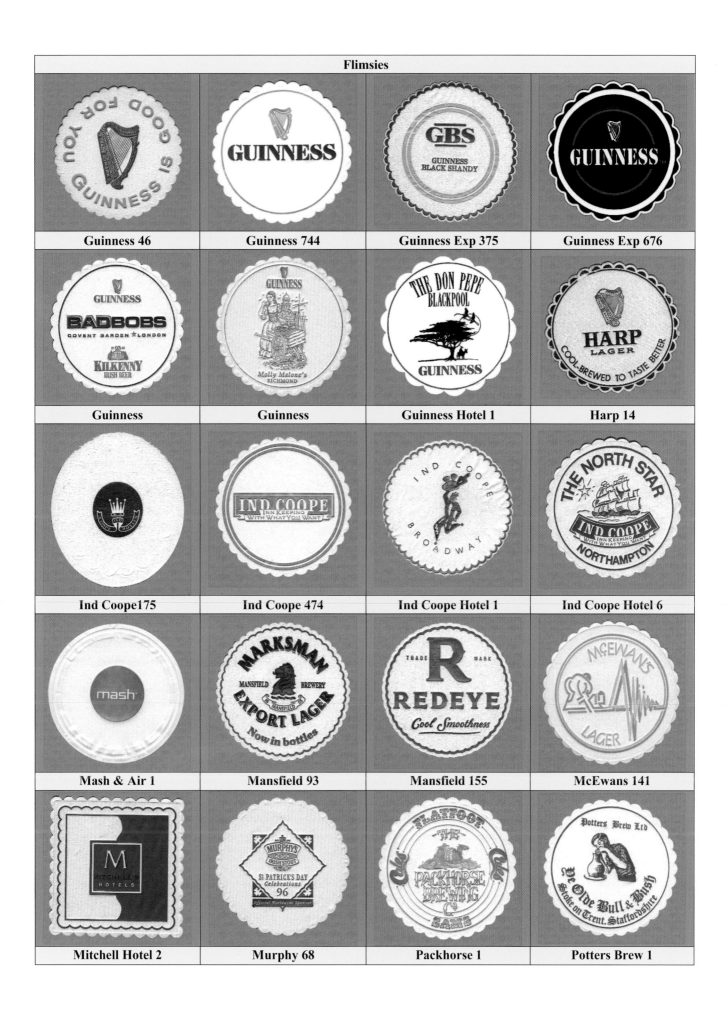

Guinness 46	Guinness 744	Guinness Exp 375	Guinness Exp 676
Guinness	Guinness	Guinness Hotel 1	Harp 14
Ind Coope175	Ind Coope 474	Ind Coope Hotel 1	Ind Coope Hotel 6
Mash & Air 1	Mansfield 93	Mansfield 155	McEwans 141
Mitchell Hotel 2	Murphy 68	Packhorse 1	Potters Brew 1

Randalls 4	S&N 39	S&N Douglas 64	Skol Holland 44
Skol Holland 116	Skol Holland 153	John Smith 108	Sam Smith 92
Swales 10	Tennents 196	Tennents 224	Tennents 226
Tennents 227	Tennents 240	Tetley 165	Tetley Hotel 1
Trough 2	Ushers (Edin) 50	Ushers 19	Ushers 20

Vaux 168	Vaux 171	Vaux 182	Vaux 184
Vaux 187	Vaux 195	Vaux 199	Vaux Hotel 2
Wards 29	Wards 36	Wards Exp 1	Whitbread 82
Whitbread 530	Whitbread 554	Whitbread Campbells 19	Whitbread Duttons 1
Whitbread House 2	Whitbread House	Youngs 93	Younger Hotel 1

Aitchison 7	Aitchison 9 (f)	Aitchison 9 (r)	Aitchison 10
Aitchison 13	Aitchison 14 (f)	Ballingall 1	Ballingall 2
Bernards 4	Bernards 5	Bernards 6 (f)	Bernards 7
Campbell, Hope & King 1	Campbell, Hope & King 3	Campbell, Hope & King 4	Campbell, Hope & King 6
Calders 41 (f)	Calders 41 (r)	Calders 44 (f)	Calders 44 (r)

Calders 46	James Deuchars 5	James Deuchars 6	James Deuchars 7
James Deuchars 8	James Deuchars 9	Robert Deuchar 9	Robert Deuchar 11
Robert Deuchar 12	Robert Deuchar 13	Robert Deuchar 15	Robert Deuchar 22
Drybroughs 2	Drybroughs 6	Drybroughs 7	Drybroughs 8
Drybroughs 9	Drybroughs 13	Drybroughs 16	Fowlers 1

Fowlers 2 (f)	Fowlers 2 (r)	Gordon & Blair 2	Gordon & Blair 3 (f)
Gordon & Blair 3 (r)	Grahams 4	Grahams 7	Grahams 10
Jeffreys 4	Jeffrey's 7	Jeffrey's 8	Lorimer & Clark 3
Lorimer & Clark 4	Lorimer & Clark 5	Mackay's 1	Maclachlans 2
Maclachlans 4	Maclay 1	Maclay 2	Maclay 7

McEwans 6	McEwans 7	McEwans 8	McEwans 9
McClennan & Urquhart 1	Morison 3	Murray 2	Murray 3
S & N 3	S & N 5	S & N 6 (f)	Steel, Coulson 3
Steel, Coulson 5	Tennents 21	Tennents 22	Tennents 23
Ushers 1	Ushers 7	Ushers 17	Utd Caledonian 1

Scottish Breweries

Utd Caledonian 3 (f)	Utd Caledonian 10	Wrights 1	Wrights 2 (r)
Wrights 3 (f)	Wrights 3 (r)	Young 1	Robert Younger 3
George Younger 7	George Younger 9	George Younger 10	Wm Younger 15
Wm Younger 16	Wm Younger 18	Wm Younger 21(f)	Wm Younger 21 (r)
Wm Younger 22 (f)	Wm Younger 22 (r)	Wm Younger 24	Wm Younger 25

37 (f)	42 (f)	55 (f)	56 (f)
58 (f)	69 (f)	73 (f)	80 (f)
86 (f)	92 (f)	97 (f)	102 (f)
107 (f)	110 (f)	112 (f)	116 (f)
117 (f)	120 (f)	124 (f)	128 (f)

130 (f)	156 (f)	160 (f)	186 (f)
347	349	350	351
362 (f)	383 (f)	399 (f)	528 (f)
601 (f)	602 (f)	603 (f)	605 (f)
625 (f)	652	657 (f)	676 (f)

712 (r)	753	948 (r)	973 (f)
987 (f)	1030 (f)	1031 (f)	1032 (f)
1033 (f)	1041 (f)	1041 (r)	1059 (f)
1069 (f)	1134 (f)	1134 (r)	1138 (f)
1138 (r)	1158 (f)	1158 (r)	1163 (r)

1179 (f)	1206 (f)	1260 (f)	1261 (f)
1262 (f)	1273 (f)	1274 (f)	1275 (f)
1276 (f)	1279 (f)	1280 (f)	1281 (f)
1282 (f)	1288 (f)	1357 (f)	1358 (f)
1402 (f)	1405 (f)	1414 (f)	1416 (f)

4	8	10 (f)	12 (f)
12 (r)	17	20	26
27	28	29	30
34 (r)	38 (f)	53	58 (f)
60	61	65	70

125 (f)	125 (r)	132 (f)	132 (r)
136	137 (f)	139 (f)	140
141 (f)	175 (r)	197 (f)	212
244	257 (f)	257 (r)	258 (r)
276	277	285	310 (r)

324 (f)	324 (r)	333 (f)	337
341	367 (f)	391	406 (r)
418 (f)	419 (f)	453 (f)	476
480 (f)	503 (f)	503 (r)	512 (f)
556	557	559 (f)	562 (f)

562 (r)	569 (f)	571	572 (f)
576	579 (r)	602	605 (f)
611	612 (f)	613 (f)	633 (f)
635	669	675	688 (f)
688 (r)	698	701 (f)	713 (f)

Guinness Export

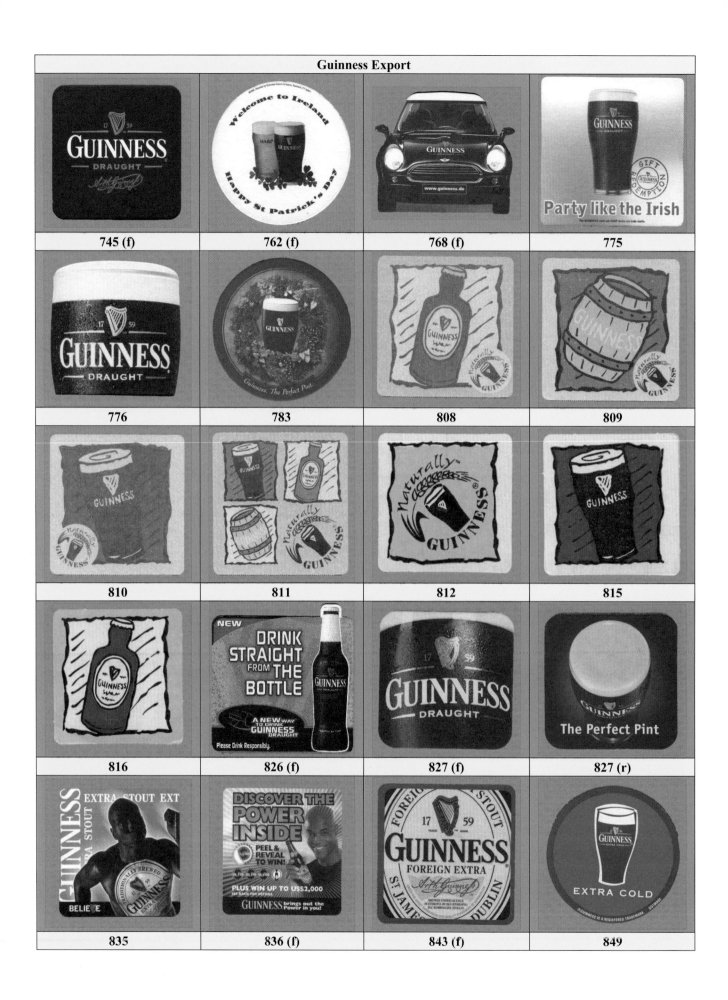

745 (f)	762 (f)	768 (f)	775
776	783	808	809
810	811	812	815
816	826 (f)	827 (f)	827 (r)
835	836 (f)	843 (f)	849

850 (f)	863 (r)	867 (r)	868 (r)
869 (r)	870 (r)	899	934 (r)
940 (f)	940 (r)	980	1025 (f)
1048 (f)	1058	1079 (f)	1082 (f)
1082 (r)	1093 (f)	1104	1106 (f)

Aitken 2	Atherton & Johnson 4 (r)	Atherton & Johnson 5 (r)	Bass 2
Bass 3	Bass 5	Bentley Yorkshire 3	Brain's 1
James Deuchar 3	Robert Deuchar 2	Duttons 4 (r)	Graham 2
Guinness Exp 1129 (f)	Guinness Exp 1129 (r)	Jeffreys 3	Jeffreys 9
Maclachlans 1	Marsh 1	Marstons 4	McEwans (unlisted)

McEwans Exp 30	McEwans Exp 42	Murray 1	Nottingham 1
Steel & Coulson 1	South London 1	Taylor 1	Tennents 7
Tennents 250	Truman 8	Worthington 5	Worthington 6
Worthington 10	Worthington Exp 18	Wm Youngers 2	Wm Youngers 3
Wm Youngers 5	Wm Youngers 6	Wm Youngers 9	Wm Youngers 12

Adnams 5 (f)	Adnams 7 (f)	Adnams 8 (f)	Allsopp 11
Almond 1	Atkinson 3	Arkells 2	Arkells 53
Barclay Perkins 14 (f)	Barclay Perkins 19	Barnsley 33	Barnsley 34
Bass 22	Bass 26	Bass 69	Bass 81 (f)
Bass 111	Bass 301 (f)	Bass 302 (f)	Bateman 40 (f)

Batham 2	Batham 3	BYB 9	Beverleys 17
Boddingtons 31 (r)	Brakspears 11 (f)	Brickwoods 11 (f)	Brown 71 (f)
Brown 103	Brutton M & T 2	Buckley 4	Burt 1
Burtonwood 14	Butler 4	Butler 16	Butler 18
Camerons 9 (f)	Carlisle 1 (f)	Castletown 8	Castletown 9 (r)

Catterall & Swarbrick 67	Catterall & Swarbrick 105	Charrington & Co 7	Charrington & Co 8
Charrington & Co 9	Charrington & Co 10	Charrington & Co 17	Charrington & Co 18
Charrington & Co 19	Cheltenham Hereford 2	Cheltenham Hereford 5	Cheltenham Hereford 6
Cheltenham Hereford 7	Cheltenham Hereford 8	Cherry 49	Clinch 2
Cobbold 8	Courage & Co 7 (f)	Dares 8	Darley 21 (r)

Davenport 7 (f)	Devenish 16 (r)	Devenish & Groves 1	Eldridge Pope 11
Eldridge Pope 25 (f)	Eldridge Pope 54 (f)	Eldridge Pope 54 (r)	Ely 6
Evan Evans Bevan 7	Everards 15 (f)	Everards 130 (f)	Everards 189 (f)
Everards 210 (f)	Felinfoel 6 (f)	Fieldings 3 (f)	Flowers 4
Flowers 11	Flowers 12	Flowers 13	Flowers 17

Flowers 19	Fremlins 7 (f)	Fremlins 7 (r)	Fremlins 8
Fremlins 9	Fullers 2	Fullers 3	Fullers 57
Fullers 117	Fullers 123	Gales 4	Gales 32 (f)
Gartside 5	Gartside 7	Gartside 8	Gibbs Mew 1
Gibbs Mew 10 (f)	Gibbs Mew 11 (f)	Green 3	Greens 5

Greenall Whitley 7	**Greenall Whitley 8**	**Greenall Whitley 172**	**Greenall Whitley 240 (f)**
Greene King 6	**Greene King 9**	**Greene King 17**	**Greene King 23**
Greene King 50	**Greene King 51**	**Greene King 52**	**Greene King 53**
Greene King 62 (f)	**Greene King 201 (r)**	**Groves 5**	**Groves & Whitnall 18**
Groves & Whitnall 19	**Guernsey 5**	**Guernsey 10 (r)**	**Guernsey 13 (r)**

Hall & Woodhouse 7	Hall & Woodhouse 23	Hall & Woodhouse 29	Hammerton 4
Hammonds 12	Hammonds 59	Hardy Hanson 6	Harp 36 (f)
Harp 109	Harp 155 (f)	Harp 203 (r)	Harp 232 (f)
Harp 236 (f)	Hemingways 12 (f)	Heys 12	Highgate 6
Highgate 7	Higsons 1	Hobsons 5	Hole 12 (f)

Home 10	Home 48	Home 49	Hook Norton 6
Hope & Anchor 4	Hope & Anchor 8	Hope & Anchor 65 (r)	Hope & Anchor 70
Hope & Anchor 71	Hope & Anchor 76	Hope & Anchor 102	Hull 22
Hull 52	Hull 53	Hull 56	Hunt 3
Hydes 3	Hydes 4	Ind Coope 14	Ind Coope 29

Ind Coope 52	Ind Coope 60	Ind Coope 245	Ind Coope 265
Ind Coope 278	Ind Coope 363	Ind Coope 406 (f)	Ind Coope FM 2 (f)
Jennings 2	Joules 2	King & Barnes 10 (f)	King & Barnes 55 (f)
Lacons 1	Lees 3	Lees 5	Maclay 44 (f)
Mackeson 11 (f)	Mackeson 31 (f)	Mackeson 31 (r)	Mackeson 44 (r)

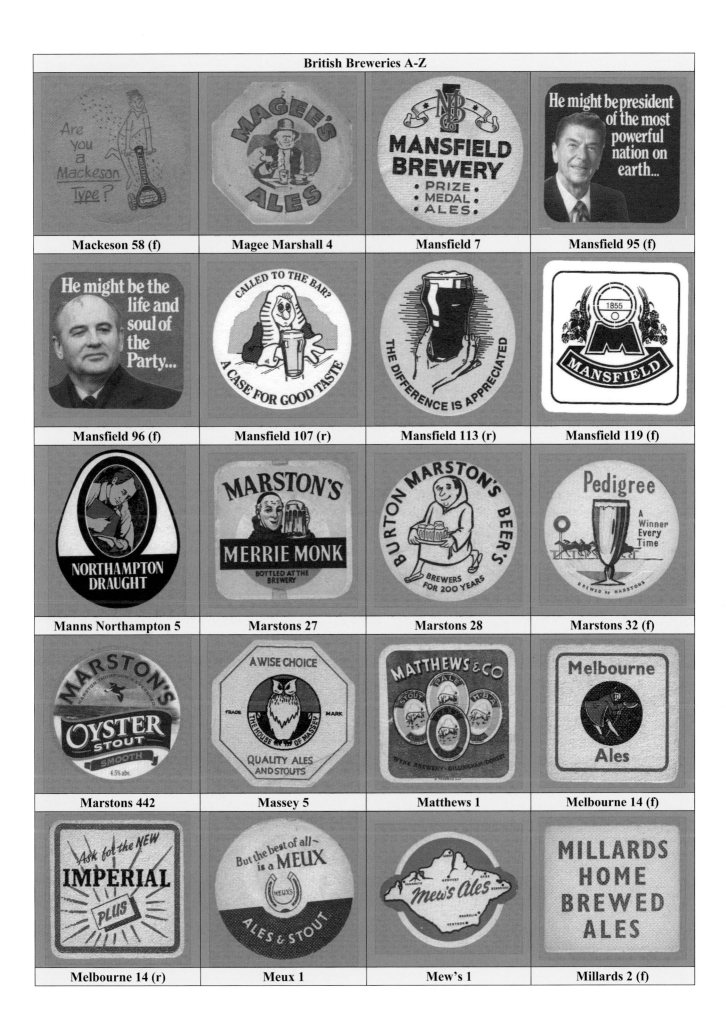

Mackeson 58 (f)	Magee Marshall 4	Mansfield 7	Mansfield 95 (f)
Mansfield 96 (f)	Mansfield 107 (r)	Mansfield 113 (r)	Mansfield 119 (f)
Manns Northampton 5	Marstons 27	Marstons 28	Marstons 32 (f)
Marstons 442	Massey 5	Matthews 1	Melbourne 14 (f)
Melbourne 14 (r)	Meux 1	Mew's 1	Millards 2 (f)

Midlands Clubs 6 (f)	Midlands Clubs 6 (r)	Mitchell's 8	Mitchell's 41 (f)
M&B 6	M&B 197	Morrell's 1	Morland 10
Morland 13	Morland 42 (f)	M & R 22	M&R 30
Murphy 90 (f)	Murphy 159 (f)	Newcastle 6	Newcastle 187
Nicholsons 4	Nimmo 5	Norman Pring 3	Northampton 1

Norwich 19 (f)	**Offilers 11**	**Offilers 28**	**Okells 6 (f)**
Plymouth 11 (f)	**Portsmouth 3**	**Ramsden 10**	**Randalls 2**
Randalls 11 (f)	**Red Tower 8**	**Red Tower 9**	**Rhymney 8**
Rhymney 32	**Ridley 1**	**Roberts 3**	**Roses 11**
Rowell 1	**Ruddles 95 (f)**	**Russells 33**	**Shepherd Neame 1**

Shepherd Neame 88 (f)	Shipstones 1	Shipstones 6	Simmonds 16
Skol 55 (f)	Skol 56 (f)	Skol 57 (f)	Skol 58 (f)
Smiles 1	John Smith 20	John Smith 157 (f)	Sam Smith 20
Sam Smith 19	Sam Smith 64	Sam Smith 144	Smithwick 53 (f)
Smithwick 120 (f)	Smithwick 139 (f)	Smithwick 145 (f)	Southams 7

Southams 8	**South Wales Clubs 3**	**Star 1 (f)**	**St. Austell 14 (f)**
St. Austell 14 (r)	**Starkey, Knight & Ford 3**	**Stones 10 (f)**	**Style & Winch 4 (f)**
Style & Winch 5 (f)	**Style & Winch 5 (r)**	**Style & Winch 6 (f)**	**Style & Winch 6 (r)**
Swales 5	**Swales 7**	**Timothy Taylors 5**	**Taylor Walker 8**
Taylor Walker 9	**Tennants 14**	**Tennants 16**	**Tetley 98 (f)**

Tetley 122 (f)	Theakston 8	Theakston 50	Thompsons 5
Thornley Kelsey 2	Threlfalls 21 (f)	Threlfalls 33 (f)	Thwaites 47 (f)
Thwaites 72 (f)	Thwaites 73	Thwaites 96 (f)	Thwaites 98 (f)
Tolly Cobbold 1	Tolly Cobbold 20 (f)	Tolly Cobbold 29 (f)	Tollmache 6
Tomson & Wotton 3 (f)	Truman 28 (r)	Truman 29 (f)	United Lancastrian 1

Ulster 2	Ushers 10	Ushers 61 (f)	Ushers 61 (r)
Vallance 2	Vaux 12	Vaux 70	Vaux 106
Vaux 137	Wadworth 10	Wadworth 11	Walker 17
Walker 30	Walker 61 (f)	Ward 8	Watney 19
Watney 27	Watney 39	Watney 40	Watney 64

Watney 10	**Watney 186**	**Webster 26**	**Webster 30**
Wells 21	**Wells 26**	**Wells 167**	**Wells 183 (f)**
Wells 231	**West Auckland 4**	**West Country 6 (f)**	**Wethered 5**
Whitaker 20	**Whitbread 5**	**Whitbread 435**	**Whitbread CE 8 (f)**
Whitbread CE 45 (f)	**Whitbread Chesters 5 (f)**	**Whitbread Wales 35**	**Wilsons 36**

Workington 7	Workington 10 (f)	Worthington 38 (f)	Worthington 38 (r)
Worthington 30	Worthington 80	Worthington 138 (f)	Wrekin 15
Yates & Jackson 5	Yorkshire Clubs 9	JJ Young 4 (f)	Youngs 7
Youngs 27 (f)	Youngs 34 (f)	Youngs 48	Youngs 69
Youngs 99	Youngs 100	Younger 209	Younger 492 (r)

Allied 5	Allsopps 18	Allsopps 19	Bass 22
Boddingtons 43 (f)	Boddingtons 44 (f)	Brown 4 (f)	Caledonian 1 (f)
Caledonian 3	Carling 86	Courage 54 (f)	Everards 1
Felinfoel 1	Flowers 1	Fullers 12 (f)	Gibbs Mew 1
Harp 76 (f)	Ind Coope 33	Mackeson 2	McEwans 1

British Brewery Export

Murphy 61 (f)	Newcastle 8	Skol 101	Skol 118
John Smith 1	John Smith 34	John Smith 66	Smithwick 1
Tennents 5	Tennents 20	Tolly Cobbold 1 (f)	Watney 61
Watneys 92	Wells 5	Whitbread 27	Whitbread 143 (f)
Whitbread 51	Worthington 7 (f)	Worthington 10 (r)	Young 2

Micro Breweries

Cotleigh 1 (f)	Cotleigh 2 (f)	Cotleigh 3 (f)	Cotleigh 6
Cotleigh 22	Cotleigh 27 (f)	Cotleigh 28 (f)	Cotleigh 29 (f)
Cotleigh 30 (f)	Cotleigh 31 (f)	Cotleigh 32 (f)	Cotleigh 33 (f)
Cotleigh 34 (f)	Cotleigh 35 (f)	Cotleigh 36 (f)	Cotleigh 50 (f)
Dark Star 3 (f)	Dark Star 4 (f)	Dark Star 5 (f)	Dark Star 6 (f)

Micro Breweries

Dark Star 7 (f)	**Dark Star 8 (f)**	**Fox & Hounds 2 (f)**	**Fox & Hounds 3 (f)**
Fox & Hounds 4 (f)	**Fox & Hounds 5 (f)**	**Fox & Hounds 6 (f)**	**Fox & Hounds 9 (f)**
Bullmastiff 1	**Bullmastiff 2**	**Bullmastiff 3**	**Bullmastiff 4**
Bruces 1 (f)	**Bruces 1 (r)**	**Bruces 3 (f)**	**Bruces 5 (f)**
Surrey Free Inns 1	**Surrey Free Inns 2**	**Surrey Free Inns 3**	**Surrey Free Inns 4**

Micro Breweries

Alcazar 1 (f)	Alford Arms 1	Alice 1 (f)	Altrincham 1
Anglo Dutch 1 (r)	Archers 1 (f)	Archers 29	Archers 32
Ashvine 1	Aviemore 1 (f)	Axe Vale 2	Baileys 1 (f)
Barking 2 (f)	Barking 2 (r)	Banks & Taylor 1	Banktop 1
Barnfield 1	Barum 1	Bates 1	Bath 1

Beartown 3	Beckets 1	Belchers 2 (f)	Berrow 1
Biddy Early 1 (f)	Big End 1 (f)	Big Lamp 1	Bitter End 1
Blackawton 6	Black Dog 1	Blackpool 1	Black Sheep 1 (f)
Black Sheep 26 (f)	Blanchfield 1	Blencowe 1 (f)	Boat 1 (f)
Bodicote1	Borve 1	Brewery on Sea 1 (f)	Branscombe Vale 2 (f)

Bridge of Allan 1	Brighton 1	Bristol 1	Burgess 1
Cairngorm 1	Cambrinus Craft 1	Canon Pyon	Castle Hotel 1
Chandlers 1	Chiltern 1 (f)	Chudley 2	Church End 18
College 1	Commercial 6 (f)	Coniston 1 (f)	Copper Dragon 1
Cotswold 1	Crouch Vale 1 (f)	Dark Star 2 (f)	Dent 1

Dent 3 (f)	**Dentons 2**	**Derwent 2**	**Doghouse 1 (f)**
Down Royal 1 (f)	**Drink Link 1 (f)**	**Dublin 1 (f)**	**Easingwold 2**
Easingwold 3	**Eastwood & Sanders 1 (f)**	**Enville 1 (f)**	**Enville 2 (f)**
Exe Valley 1 (f)	**Failsworth 1**	**Fernandes 3 (f)**	**Fleece & Firkin 1 (f)**
Flag 1	**Four Keys 1 (f)**	**Foxfield 10 (f)**	**Franciscan Well 1 (f)**

Freedom 4	Frog Island 1 (f)	Fyne Ales 1 (f)	Glenny 1 (f)
Goddard 5 (f)	Goff 2 (f)	Golden Hill 23 (f)	Goose Eye 1
Goose Eye 6	Gribble Inn 1	Gwynedd 1	Hadrian 3 (f)
Hadrian & Border 1 (f)	Hambelton 3 (f)	Hambleton 3 (r)	Hardington 1 (f)
Harty 1 (f)	Harviestoun 1 (f)	Hawkhead 1 (f)	Hawthorn 1 (f)

Hawthorne 1	Heather Ales 1 (f)	Herald 1	Heritage 1
Heritage 4	Hopback 1	Hoskins 5 (r)	Hoskins 22 (f)
Houston 3 (f)	Homecoming	Hull 5 (f)	Inn off the Green 1 (f)
Inveralmond 1	Islay 1 (f)	Isle of Skye 2 (r)	Itchen Valley 1 (f)
Jarrow 1 (f)	Jolly Boat 4 (f)	Jolly Roger 9 (f)	Kemptown 1

Keystone 1 (f)	**Kings Ale 1 (f)**	**Larkins 1 (f)**	**Lastingham 1 (f)**
Leaking Boot 1	**Ledbury 1**	**Leyland 1 (f)**	**Lions Original 1**
Litchborough 6	**Liverpool 1 (f)**	**Longstone 1**	**Maguires 1 (f)**
Malton 1	**Malvern Chase 1 (f)**	**Marston Moor 7**	**Martin 1**
Mauldons 1 (f)	**Mayhems 1 (f)**	**Mendip 1**	**McGuiness 1**

Mickles 1	Mighty Oak 1	Millennium 2	Minera 2
Minerva 1 (f)	Moles 10	Moorhouses 11 (f)	New Fenmor Arms 1
Newby Wyke 1	New Forest 1 (f)	Newmans 1	Nix Wincott 1
Nix Wincott 2	Northumberland 1 (f)	North Cornwall 1	North & East Riding 1 (r)
Oakleaf 3 (f)	Oakwell 1	Old Bear 1	Old Bear 2

Old Chidham 1 (f)	**Old Mill 1 (f)**	**Old Swan 1**	**Orkney 3**
Orkney 4	**Ossett 1 (f)**	**Otter 1 (f)**	**Otter 1 (r)**
Otter 3 (f)	**Owl 1 (f)**	**Packhorse 2 (f)**	**Palmer 6**
Parker 2 (f)	**Pembroke 1**	**Pembrokeshire 1**	**Penrhos 3**
Pilgrim 1 (f)	**Priory 3 (f)**	**Poole 1 (f)**	**Purple Moose 1**

Micro Breweries

Micro Breweries

 RECTORY ALES — BREWED & CASKED IN PLUMPTON GREEN, SUSSEX	RED KITE BREWERY — FLYER — WITH MALT HOPS & WATER	RED KITE BREWERY — Original — WITH MALT HOPS & WATER	Ribblesdale Arms — Gisburn — Nr. Clitheroe — Lancashire
Rectory 1 (f)	**Red Kite 1**	**Red Kite 2**	**Ribblesdale 1 (f)**
ROBINWOOD BREWERY — TODMORDEN YORKSHIRE — CASK CONDITIONED ALES	AULD REEKIE ALE — THE ROSE St BREWERY	ROSS — CASNEWYDD — 3.5% — Ross Brewing Co. Newport Brewhouse, Market Street, Newport NP1 Tel: (01633) 212186	COMBE'S OWN — EARTHQUAKE ALE — EARTHQUAKE ALE
Robinwood 1	**Rose St 1 (f)**	**Ross 1**	**Royal Hotel 1 (f)**
SALAMANDER — BREWING COMPANY	BREWED IN SELBY ENGLAND — BRAHMS & LISZT — SPECIAL PALE ALE	PLAXTOL (0732) 810222	SPINNING DOG BREWERY — "A BEER WITH A BITE" — ENQUIRIES TEL 01432 342125 — www.spinningdogbrewery.co.uk — Real Ales at Real Prices
Salamander 3	**Selby 3**	**Sevenoaks 1**	**Spinning Dog 1**
THE STAR & TIPSY TOAD BREWERY — St Peter's Village — Jersey C.I. — Tel 0534 485556 — TIPSY TOAD Brewery	Blow Job — 3.7% A.B.V. — From Knottingley the home of Glass for 126 years — STEAMPACKET BREWERY	"A GATHERING — Ginger Minge — A.B.V. 4.5% — OF WOMEN" — THE STEAMPACKET BREWERY 01977 674176	SUMMERSKILLS — BIGBURY BEST BITTER — EST. 1983
Star & Tipsy Toad 1	**Steampacket 41 (f)**	**Steampacket 49 (f)**	**Summerskills 1**
SWANNELLS — SWANNELLS BREWERY LTD KINGS LANGLEY HERTS 65076 — NUMBERS FARM, STATION ROAD, KINGS LANGLEY	naturally cloudy, naturally brewed for your enjoyment. Naturally fresh, naturally — LES FRÈRES — Swale Brewery — Brasserie Thiriez — DE LA BIÈRE	Swansea Brewing SBC Company — Brewed at The Joiners Bishopston	TATE'S TRADITIONAL BITTER — THE TATE BREWERY LIMITED
Swannells 1 (f)	**Swale 1**	**Swansea 2 (f)**	**Tate 1 (f)**

Teme Valley 1 (f)	Three Tuns 2 (f)	Tigertops 3	Titanic 4
Tomlinsons 1	Trough 4 (f)	Trough 35	Trough 36
Trough 39	Uley 2	Vale 1	Valhalla 1 (f)
Ventnor 1 (f)	Victoria 3 (f)	Victoria 4	Viking 1
Warwickshire 1	Watkins 2	West Berkshire 2	West Crown 1

Westmorland 1	West Riding 1	West Yorks Micros 1 (f)	Whittingtons 1 (f)
Wicked Hathern 1 (f)	Wickwar 1 (f)	Wickwar 7	Wiltshire 1 (f)
Windsor 1	Winter's 1	Wold Top 1	Wolf 1
Wood's 3 (f)	Wooden Hand 1 (f)	Woodforde's 7 (f)	Woodlands 1
Wychwood 3	Wye Valley 12 (r)	Wylam 1	Wyre Piddle 1

Christmas Issues

\n**Arkells 64**	\n**Banks 27 (f)**	\n**Carling 212 (r)**	\n**Derwent 8 (f)**
\n**Everards 223 (f)**	\n**Fox & Hounds 8 (f)**	\n**Guinness 830 (f)**	\n**Guinness 1011(f)**
\n**Guinness 1020 (f)**	\n**Guinness 1254 (f)**	\n**Harp 131**	\n**Holdens 19 (r)**
\n**McEwans Exp 37**	\n**Murphy 80**	\n**Murphy Exp 80**	\n**Murphy Exp 81**
\n**John Smith 13 (r)**	\n**John Smith Exp 4**	\n**Webster 43**	\n**Whitbread Campbell 45**

St. Patrick's Day / Halloween

Beamish Exp 7 (f)	Guinness 733	Guinness 756	Guinness 775
Guinness Exp 413 (f)	Guinness Exp 414 (f)	Guinness Exp 895	Guinness Exp 902 (f)
Guinness Exp 943 (f)	Guinness Exp 944 (f)	Guinness Exp 951	Guinness Exp 986 (f)
Guinness Exp 996 (f)	Guinness Exp 1055 (f)	Guinness Exp 1075	Guinness JA 44 (r)
Irish Ale Exp 5 (f)	Irish Ale Exp 6 (f)	Murphy Exp 77	Murphy Exp 78

Aitken 3	Banks 210	Banks 226 (f)	Courage 12
Courage 80	Fullers 21 (f)	Fullers 21 (r)	Greene King 180 (f)
Greene King 221 (f)	Jennings 9	John Smith 196 (f)	Wells 214 (f)
Wells 214 (r)	Wells 223 (r)	Whitbread 446 (f)	Youngs 98

Nations flags

154

Sport			

Buckley 44 (f)	Camerons 75	Carling 424 (f)	Charrington Utd 28
Guinness 406 (f)	Guinness 915 (f)	Guinness 1354 (f)	Guinness Exp 851 (f)
Harp Exp 85	Harp Exp 86	Higsons 107 (f)	Smithwick 19 (f)
Smithwick 20 (f)	Smithwick 21 (f)	Smithwick 22 (f)	Taylor Walker 4
Tennents 122 (f)	Tennents 238 (f)	Ushers (Edin) 16	Younger 141

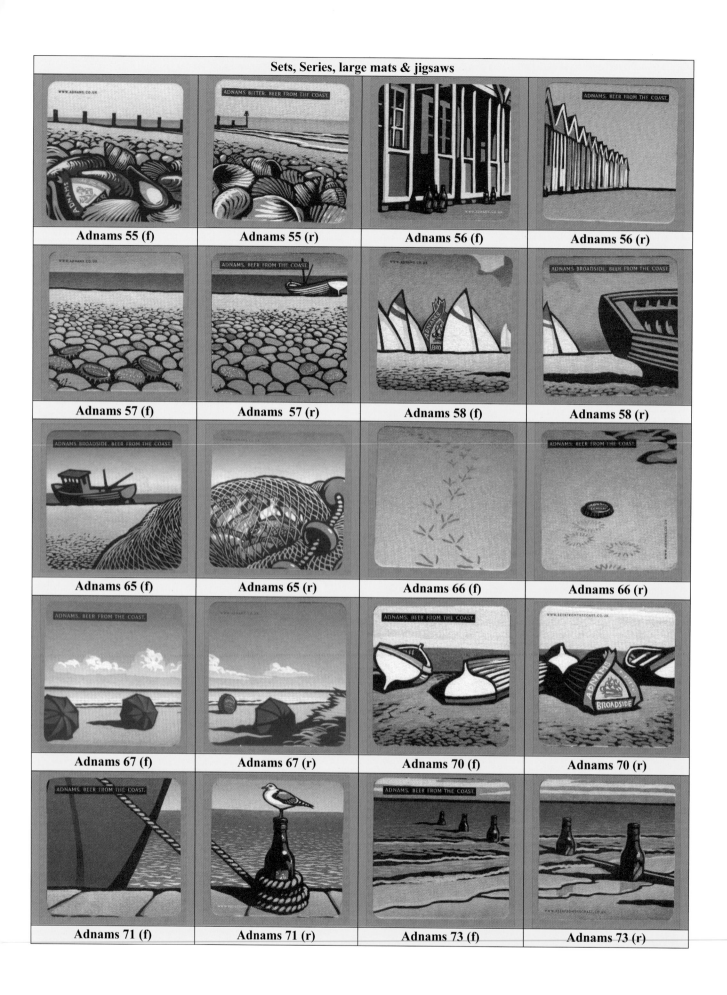

Adnams 55 (f)	Adnams 55 (r)	Adnams 56 (f)	Adnams 56 (r)
Adnams 57 (f)	Adnams 57 (r)	Adnams 58 (f)	Adnams 58 (r)
Adnams 65 (f)	Adnams 65 (r)	Adnams 66 (f)	Adnams 66 (r)
Adnams 67 (f)	Adnams 67 (r)	Adnams 70 (f)	Adnams 70 (r)
Adnams 71 (f)	Adnams 71 (r)	Adnams 73 (f)	Adnams 73 (r)

Adnams 41 (f)	Adnams 42 (f)	Adnams 43 (f)	Adnams 38 (f)
Thwaites 67 (f)	Thwaites 68 (f)	Thwaites 69 (f)	Thwaites 70 (f)
Marstons 379 (f)	Marstons 380 (f)	Marstons 381 (f)	Marstons 382 (f)
Marstons 383 (f)	Marstons 384 (f)	Ringwood 24 (f)	Ringwood 23 (f)
Dwan 5 (f)	Dwan 6 (f)	Dwan 7 (f)	Dwan 8 (f)

Elgood 26 (r)	Elgood 27 (r)	Elgood 28 (r)	Elgood 29 (r)
Elgood 30 (r)	Elgood 31 (r)	Elgood 32 (r)	Elgood 33 (r)
Elgood 34 (r)	Elgood 35 (r)	Tetley 149 (f)	Tetley 159 (f)
Coniston 29 (f)	Coniston 30 (f)	Youngers 526 (f)	Youngers 525 (f)
Coniston 32 (f)	Coniston 31 (f)	Youngers 528 (f)	Youngers 527 (f)

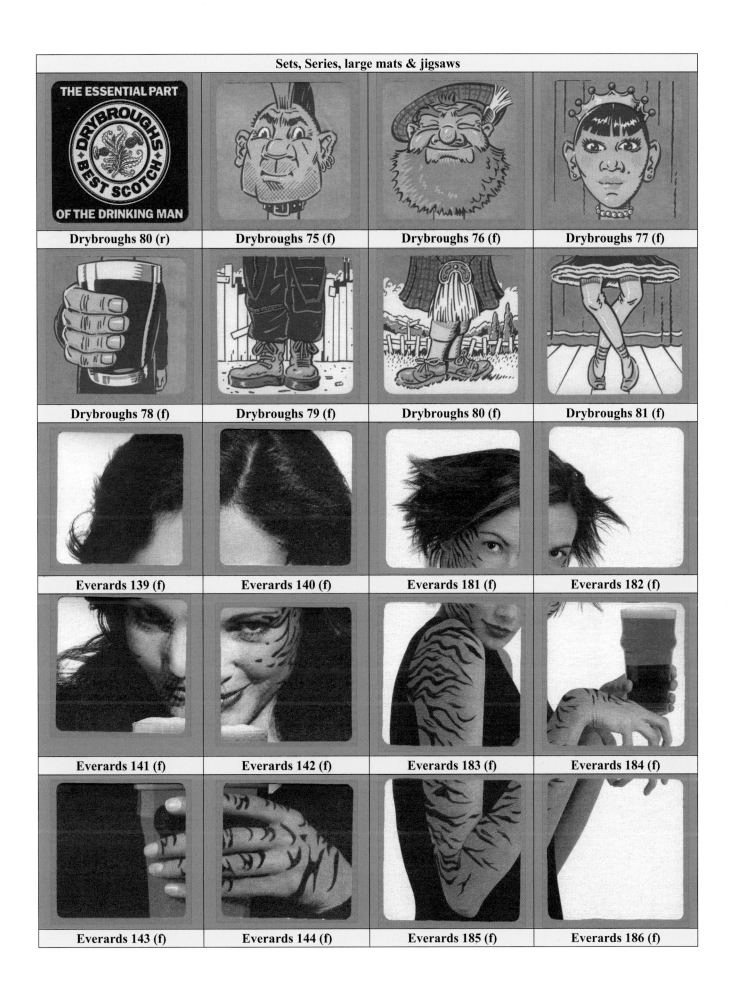

Drybroughs 80 (r)	Drybroughs 75 (f)	Drybroughs 76 (f)	Drybroughs 77 (f)
Drybroughs 78 (f)	Drybroughs 79 (f)	Drybroughs 80 (f)	Drybroughs 81 (f)
Everards 139 (f)	Everards 140 (f)	Everards 181 (f)	Everards 182 (f)
Everards 141 (f)	Everards 142 (f)	Everards 183 (f)	Everards 184 (f)
Everards 143 (f)	Everards 144 (f)	Everards 185 (f)	Everards 186 (f)

Sets, Series, large mats & jigsaws			
Thwaites 75 (f)	Thwaites 76 (f)	Thwaites 77 (f)	Thwaites 78 (f)
Charles Wells 88 (r)	Charles Wells 88 (f)	Charles Wells 89 (f)	Charles Wells 90 (f)
Charles Wells 91 (f)	Charles Wells 92 (f)	Charles Wells 93 (f)	Charles Wells 94 (f)
Charles Wells 95 (f)	Charles Wells 96 (f)	Charles Wells 97 (f)	Charles Wells 98 (f)
Charles Wells 99 (f)	John Smith 152 (r)	John Smith 153 (r)	John Smith 154 (r)

Shepherd Neame168 (r)	Shepherd Neame 168(f)	Shepherd Neame 169 (f)	Shepherd Neame 170 (f)
Shepherd Neame 171 (f)	Shepherd Neame 172 (f)	Shepherd Neame 174 (f)	Shepherd Neame 175 (f)
Shepherd Neame 176 (f)	Shepherd Neame 177 (f)	Shepherd Neame 178 (f)	Shepherd Neame 179 (f)
Shepherd Neame 180 (f)	Shepherd Neame 181 (f)	Shepherd Neame 208 (f)	Shepherd Neame 209 (f)
Shepherd Neame 210 (f)	Shepherd Neame 211 (f)	Shepherd Neame 212 (f)	Shepherd Neame 213 (f)

Guinness 927 (f)	Guinness 927 (r)	Guinness 928 (f)	Guinness 928 (r)
Guinness 1222 (f)	Guinness 1223 (f)	Guinness 815 (f)	Guinness 816 (f)
Guinness 1224 (f)	Guinness 1225 (f)	Guinness 817 (f)	Guinness 818 (f)
Brains 174 (f)	Brains 175 (f)	Ind Coope 422 (f)	Ind Coope 423 (f)
Brains 176 (f)	Brains 177 (f)	Ind Coope 424 (f)	Ind Coope 425 (f)

Carling 110 (f)	Carling 111 (f)	Harp 73	Harp 74
Carling 112 (f)	Carling 113 (f)	Skol 96	Skol 97

Hall & Woodhouse 95-102 (f)

Alloa 14 (f)	Alloa 15 (f)	Marstons 45	Marstons 46

163

John Smith 163 (f)	John Smith 164 (f)	John Smith 165 (f)	
John Smith 162 (f)	John Smith 167 (f)	John Smith 166 (f)	Freedom 3 (f)
Arkell 37	Arkell 42	Arkell 47	Arkell 48
S&N 75	S&N 76	S&N 77	S&N 79
Randalls 32	Randalls 33	Randalls 34	Randalls 35

371 (f)	372 (f)	373 (f)	374 (f)
375 (f)	376 (f)	377 (f)	378 (f)
386 (f)	387 (f)	389 (f)	390 (f)
391 (f)	392 (f)	394 (f)	399 (f)
400 (f)	401 (f)	402 (f)	404 (f)

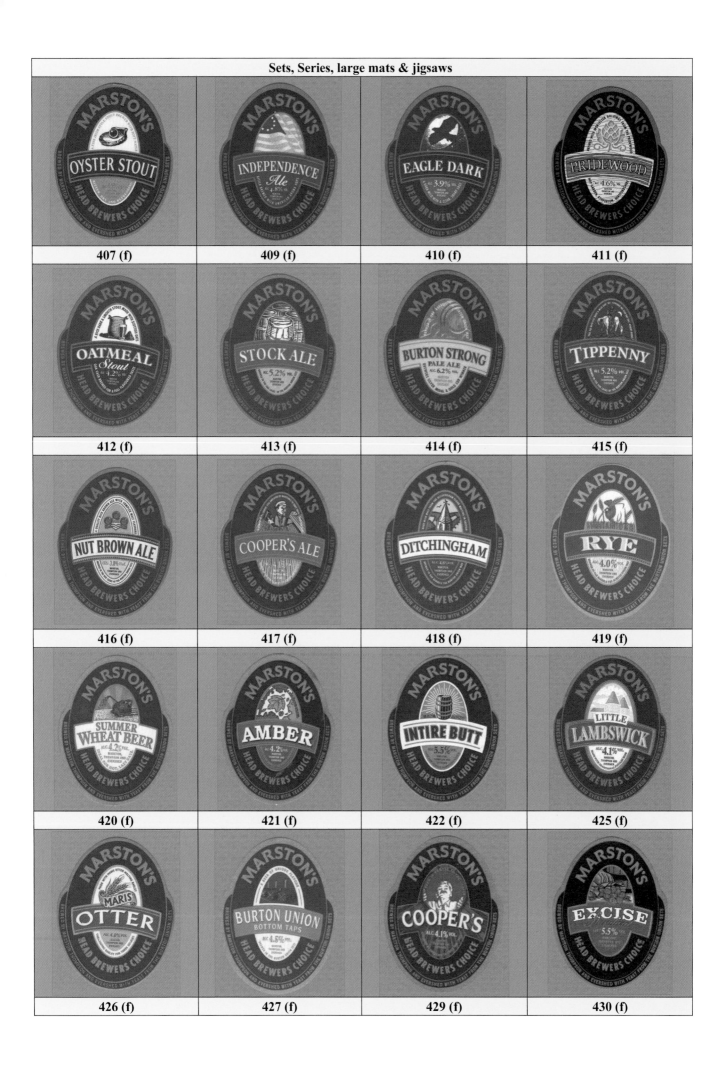

407 (f)	409 (f)	410 (f)	411 (f)
412 (f)	413 (f)	414 (f)	415 (f)
416 (f)	417 (f)	418 (f)	419 (f)
420 (f)	421 (f)	422 (f)	425 (f)
426 (f)	427 (f)	429 (f)	430 (f)

431 (f)	433 (f)	434 (f)	435 (f)
Young 70 (f)	Young 71 (f)	Young 72 (f)	Young 73 (f)
Young 74 (f)	Young 75 (f)	Young 76 (f)	Young 77 (f)
Bass 155 (f)	Bass 157 (f)	Bass 158 (f)	Bass 162 (f)
Manns 34 (f)	Manns 34 (r)	Manns 36 (f)	Manns 37 (r)

McMullen 16 (f)	McMullen 17 (f)	McMullen 18 (f)	McMullen 19 (f)
McMullen 20 (f)	McMullen 21 (f)	McMullen 22 (f)	McMullen 23 (f)
McMullen 24 (f)	McMullen 25 (f)	McMullen 26 (f)	McMullen 27 (f)
McMullen 31 (f)	McMullen 32 (f)	McMullen 33 (f)	McMullen 34 (f)
McMullen 35 (f)	McMullen 36 (f)	McMullen 37 (f)	McMullen 38 (f)

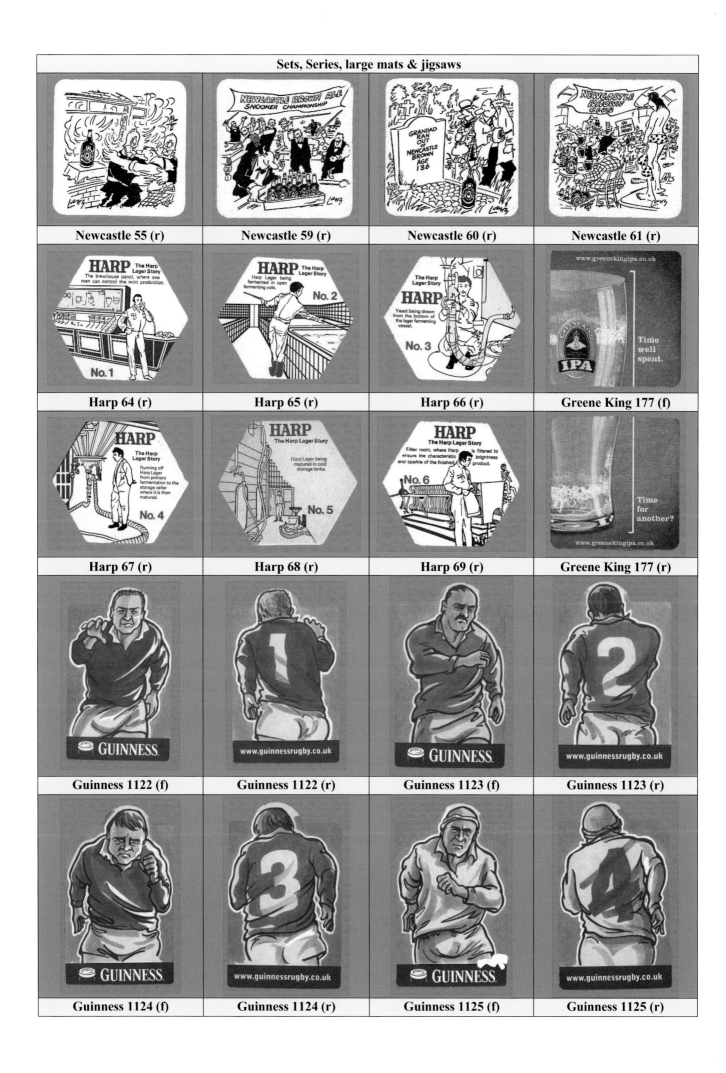

Newcastle 55 (r)	Newcastle 59 (r)	Newcastle 60 (r)	Newcastle 61 (r)
Harp 64 (r)	Harp 65 (r)	Harp 66 (r)	Greene King 177 (f)
Harp 67 (r)	Harp 68 (r)	Harp 69 (r)	Greene King 177 (r)
Guinness 1122 (f)	Guinness 1122 (r)	Guinness 1123 (f)	Guinness 1123 (r)
Guinness 1124 (f)	Guinness 1124 (r)	Guinness 1125 (f)	Guinness 1125 (r)

Sets, Series, large mats & jigsaws

Sets, Series, large mats & jigsaws			
 Greenalls 153 (f)	Greenalls 158 (f)	Greenalls 159 (f)	Greenalls 160 (f)
 Newcastle 177 (f)		 Newcastle 178 (f)	
 Watneys 232 (f)		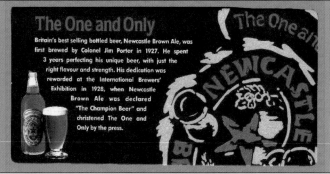 Watneys 240 (f)	
 Murphy Exp 7 (Gatefold mat)		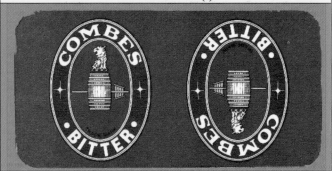	
 Wadworth 89 (r)		 Wadworth 90 (r)	

Smithwick 254 (f)

Smithwick 254 (r)

Smithwick 255 (r)

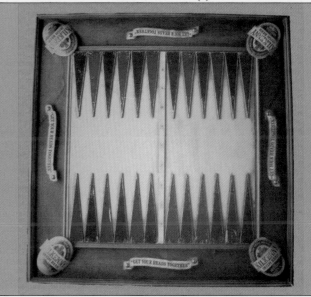

Smithwick 256 (r)

Smithwick 257 (f)

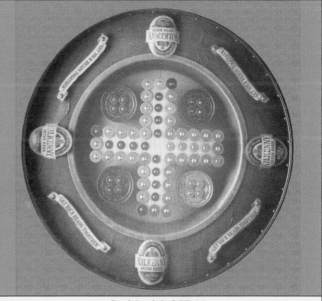

Smithwick 257 (r)

Scottish & Newcastle 7

Ushers (Edin) 9

Border 66

Ruddles 102 (f)

Threlfalls 39

Cobb 5

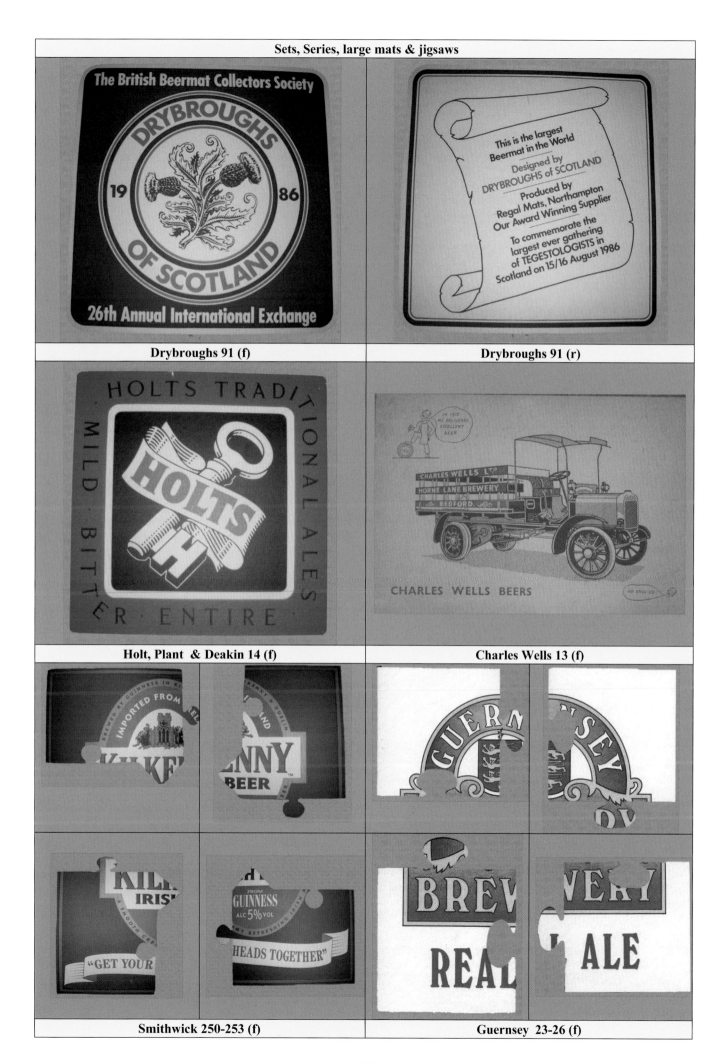

Drybroughs 91 (f)   Drybroughs 91 (r)

Holt, Plant & Deakin 14 (f)   Charles Wells 13 (f)

Smithwick 250-253 (f)   Guernsey 23-26 (f)

Drivers Please don't have one for the road and risk your licence — We want to see you more than once a year	MOTORISTS PLEASE — NO OVERDRINKING — Issued by the Brewing Industry in the interest of road safety	Think before you drink before you drive — Be sensible, be safe. — Issued by the Brewing Industry in the interest of road safety	A drink/driving conviction may now mean a 1-3 years ban, or longer plus up to a £1000 fine, 6 months in jail, or both — Be sensible, be safe. — Issued by the Brewing Industry in the interest of road safety
DW-1	**DW-2**	**DW-3**	**DW-5**
Think before you drink before you drive — BANNED YOU COULD BE ONE DRINK AWAY — Issued by the Brewing Industry in the interest of road safety	Keep your Wheels! — A drink/driving conviction may now mean 1-3 years ban, up to £1000 fine, 6 months in jail and costly problems with your insurance — Issued by the Brewing Industry in the interest of road safety	THINK BEFORE YOU DRINK BEFORE YOU DRIVE — Driving licence	OVER 80 IN THE BREATH TEST AND YOU'RE ON A LOSER — Issued by the Brewing Industry in the interest of road safety
DW-6	**DW-7**	**DW-8**	**DW-9**
EPHRAIMS ALES — EST 1778 — EPHRAIMS ALES	EPHRAIM MONK ALES — ESTABLISHED 1778 — BREWERY	THE WOOLPACK BECKINDALE	CWM DERWEN ALES — BRAGDY CWMDERI BREWERY
DIXIELAND CENTRAL PIER — JIM BOWEN — BLACKPOOL	CHURCHILL EST. 1834 STRONG ALE WHITARD & COMPANY	Est. 1903 DOYLES EXTRA SMOOTH ALE 80/-	SHIRES BREWERY — BORSETSHIRE ALES
NEWTON AND RIDLEY BEST BITTER	CORONATION STREET THE ROVERS RETURN™ WEATHERFIELD LANCASHIRE — NEWTON AND RIDLEY THE LANCASHIRE BREWERS	Rovers Return Coronation Street — Newton and Ridley Newton and Ridley Newton and Ridley BEST BITTER	Newton & Ridley Rovers Return

Miscellaneous

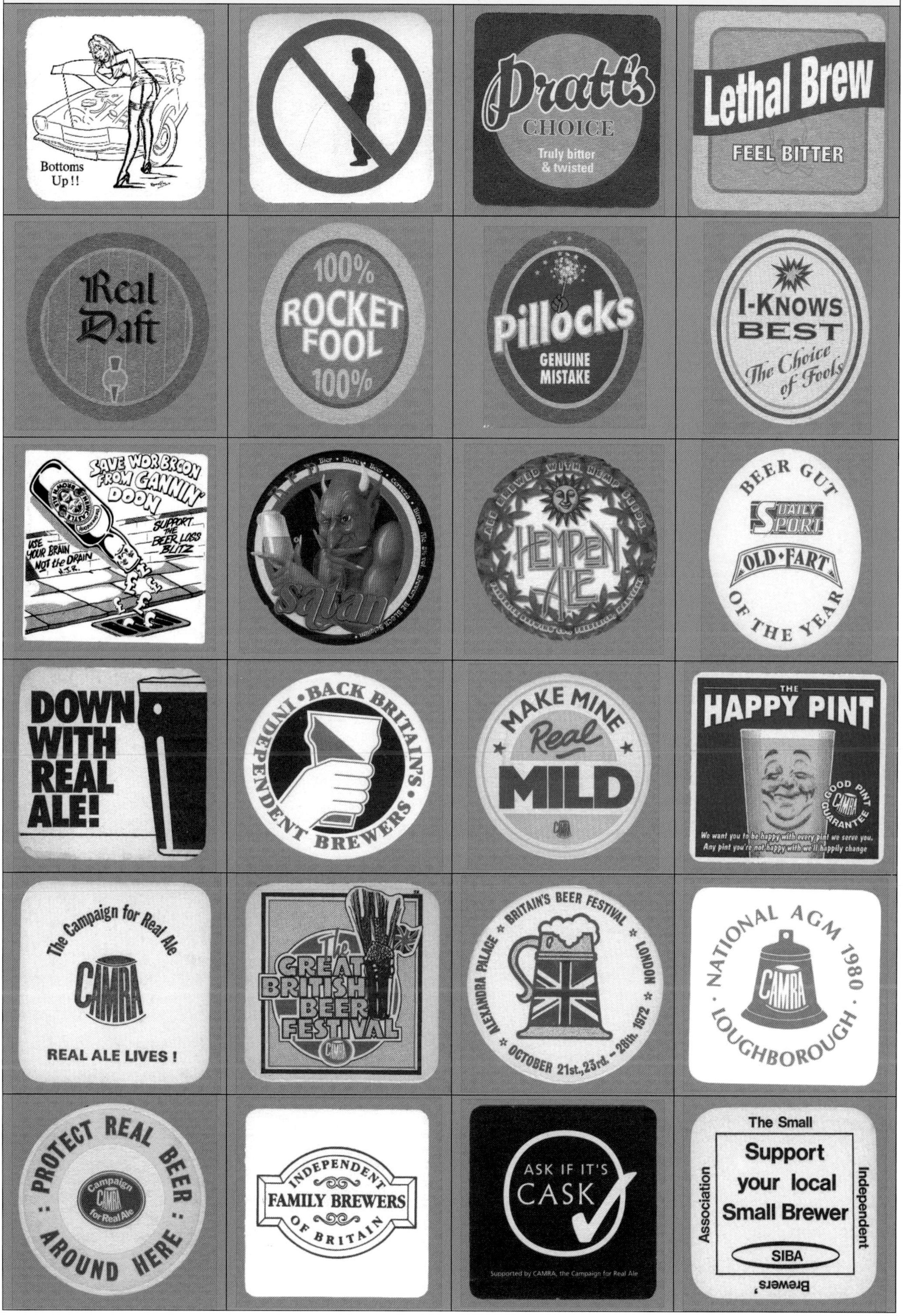

BEER MAT APPEAL

This is an appeal on behalf of some beer mats, please listen to their plight.

DEAR BEER DRINKERS.

LIFE FOR US BEERMATS IS SLIM – A FEW HOURS, A COUPLE OF DAYS AT BEST. THEN A QUICK FLIP AND FOLD FROM A CUTE BARMAID, AND OFF TO THE BIG RECYCLING BIN IN THE SKY.

ALL WE ASK BEFORE WE POP OFF IS; LET US TASTE SOMETHING. NEXT TIME YOU'RE SAVOURING YOUR PINT OF McEWAN'S, AND YOU SEE A TASTY DRIP ROLLING DOWN THE GLASS, HOLD YOURSELF BACK FROM LICKING IT.

LET US TASTE THE REAL McEWAN'S.

CHEERS, AND ENJOY.

THE REAL

USING US BEERMATS TO STOP TABLES WOBBLING?

WHAT DID WE EVER DO TO YOU?

BEERMATS HAVE DREAMS TOO YOU KNOW. WE LIVE FOR WOBBLY TABLES. THEY GIVE US A SLIVER OF HOPE.

WE LONG FOR THE DAY THAT A HAND WILL PLACE A PINT OF McEWAN'S ON US. THE TABLE WILL ROCK, LEFT, THEN RIGHT, THEN LEFT AGAIN. A DROP OF McEWAN'S WILL ROLL DOWN THE GLASS. AND FOR ONCE IN OUR PITIFUL LIVES, WE'LL ACTUALLY GET TO TASTE SOMETHING...

LET THE DREAM LIVE.

LET THE TABLE WOBBLE.

THE REAL

PLEASE LET A TASTY DROP OF McEWAN'S SPILL ON ME.

I'LL LET YOU TRIPLE FLIP AND CATCH ME IN FRONT OF THE BLONDE BY THE BAR.

THE REAL

WE BEERMATS DON'T GET PAID YOU KNOW.

WE DO IT FOR LOVE.

PLEASE, SPILL A TASTY DRIBBLE OF McEWAN'S ON ME.

THE REAL

"I HAD A DROP ONCE... IT WAS THE GREATEST DAY OF MY LIFE."

"IF YOU THINK IT'S BAD BEING GUINNLESS...YOU WANT TO TRY THIS FOR A CAPER!"

"OOOH, FOR A CLUMSY DRINKER."